South Bend Ghosts

& Other Northern Indiana Haunts

Stephen Osborne

Schiffer Publishing Ltd

Dedication

To the big three:
My mother, Frank, and Jadzia the Wonder Dog.
I also dedicate this to the memory of my father.

Disclaimer:
Many of the places mentioned in this book are on private property. You should never attempt to investigate *any* haunted location without first gaining proper permission. Failure to do so could result in an arrest for trespassing.

Schiffer Books are available at special discounts for bulk purchases for sales promotions or premiums. Special editions, including personalized covers, corporate imprints, and excerpts can be created in large quantities for special needs. For more information contact the publisher:

Schiffer Publishing Ltd.
4880 Lower Valley Road
Atglen, PA 19310
Phone: (610) 593-1777; Fax: (610) 593-2002
E-mail: Info@schifferbooks.com

For the largest selection of fine reference books on this and related subjects,
please visit our web site at: **www.schifferbooks.com**
We are always looking for people to write books on new and related subjects.
If you have an idea for a book please contact us at the above address.

This book may be purchased from the publisher.
Include $5.00 for shipping.
Please try your bookstore first.
You may write for a free catalog.

In Europe, Schiffer books are distributed by
Bushwood Books
6 Marksbury Ave.
Kew Gardens
Surrey TW9 4JF England
Phone: 44 (0) 20 8392-8585; Fax: 44 (0) 20 8392-9876
E-mail: info@bushwoodbooks.co.uk
Website: www.bushwoodbooks.co.uk
Free postage in the U.K., Europe; air mail at cost.

Other Schiffer Books on Related Subjects
Haunted Indianapolis: And Other Indiana Ghost Stories, 978-0-7643-2747-6, $14.95
Strange Indiana Monsters, 0-7643-2608-2, $12.95
Greetings from Indianapolis, 978-0-7643-2629-5, $24.95

Copyright © 2009 by Stephen Osborne
Library of Congress Control Number: 2008942470

All rights reserved. No part of this work may be reproduced or used in any form or by any means—graphic, electronic, or mechanical, including photocopying or information storage and retrieval systems—without written permission from the publisher.

The scanning, uploading and distribution of this book or any part thereof via the Internet or via any other means without the permission of the publisher is illegal and punishable by law. Please purchase only authorized editions and do not participate in or encourage the electronic piracy of copyrighted materials.

"Schiffer," "Schiffer Publishing Ltd. & Design," and the "Design of pen and ink well" are registered trademarks of Schiffer Publishing Ltd.

Designed by Mark David Bowyer
Type set in Bard / NewsGothic BT

ISBN: 978-0-7643-3199-2
Printed in the United States of America

Contents

Introduction 5

Chapter One: Tippecanoe Place Restaurant 7

Chapter Two: Are They Haunted–Or Not? 21
    Primrose Road 21
    Adams Street Cemetery 25

Chapter Three: Dierdre's Ghost 29

Chapter Four: The Gipper & Notre Dame's Ghosts 33
    The Ghosts of Washington Hall 33
    The Spirits of St. Mary's College 39

Chapter Five: On the Trail of Ghosts 43
    My Night With South Bend Paranormal Task Force 43

Chapter Six: Grandmother's House 51

Chapter Seven: Sister of Mercy 57

Chapter Eight: The House on Somerset 61

Chapter Nine: A Ghost Tour of Northern Indiana 69
    A La Porte Haunting 76

Chapter Ten: The Tale of the Black Widow 81
    Belle Gunness and the Paranormal 86
    Becca's Story 90

Contents

Chapter Eleven: Jailhouse & Graveyard Specters 93
  Crown Point Jail 93
  The Gypsies Graveyard 95

Chapter Twelve: Ghostly Theatres, Cemeteries, & Bridges 97
  Bristol Opera House 97
  Little Egypt Cemetery & Troll Bridge 99

Chapter Thirteen: Small City Haunts 101
  Blue Cast Sanitarium 101
  The Small, Haunted City of Kendallville 102
  Myths & Legends of Rochester 104

Chapter Fourteen: The Moody Lights 107

Chapter Fifteen: The Lady in White 109
  And Other Hammond Ghosts 109

Chapter Sixteen: More than a Home 115
  The Speakeasy 115
  The Kaske House 116
  The Inn at Aberdeen 117

Chapter Seventeen: The House of Evil 125

Chapter Eighteen: Diana of the Dunes 135

Chapter Nineteen: Big City Haunts 141
  Haunted Huntington 141
  The Ghosts of Fort Wayne 143

Chapter Twenty: The Mean Deer 147
  A Family's Ongoing Saga 147

Conclusion: A Personal Brush with the Paranormal 151

Bibliography 155

Places Index 157

Introduction

Located at the southernmost turn of the St. Joseph River (giving the city its name), South Bend has a population of around 108,000. It's the county seat of St. Joseph County and the fourth largest city in Indiana. In 1679 famed explorer, Robert Lasalle, traveled through the area, claiming it for France. Soon other European nations were vying for control of the St. Joseph River Valley. In the 1700s the area was populated with Indian tribes such as the Potawatomi and Miami as well as French and British explorers. Fur traders began to settle here, and soon families were arriving from the east, calling St. Joseph Valley their home. The area steadily grew and South Bend officially became a city in 1865. The river access brought the city some heavy industrial development. The Studebaker plant was based in South Bend.

The population of 108,000, of course, counts *only* the living. Some residents seem to find the city they know and love too wonderful to leave—even after death. They are still here...in the shadows. They can be found hovering around the cemeteries where they were buried, or they might walk the halls of the dormitories they lived in while students. On moonlit nights you can spy them standing by disused train tracks or riding white horses up the steps of Washington Hall at the University of Notre Dame. Some are seen as they were in their last moments of their lives, hanging from a bell tower or staring up from a watery grave.

Ghost stories are told in every culture in every continent across the globe. They provide us with enjoyable shivers. They are, in a way, mental roller coaster rides. We enjoy the goose bumps they give us and the way they make our hearts beat just a little faster, but we keep the thought in the back of our minds that such things can't really exist. They are stories, and that is all. We are really safe in the darkness...aren't we? But then there's that shadow in the corner that shouldn't be there, and the footsteps coming down the hall when you know you're alone in the building...

These are tales to be told around the campfire. They are legends to be enjoyed with your friends on those dark nights when the subject of ghosts and the paranormal come up. Some have a historical basis; others are closer to urban legends. I hope they raise a goose pimple or two. If you hear ghostly footsteps or banging on the walls while you're reading, you may want to ignore the sounds—because investigating them might bring you face-to-face with one of the specters from these pages...

There are several different types of hauntings. A *residual haunt* is a little scene out of the past, being played over and over again. The spirit doesn't interact with the living. Indeed, it doesn't even know anyone is watching. Residual haunts can be viewed as a fracture in time, playing over and over again like a tape on a loop. Sometimes they happen at a certain time every night, or on the anniversary of whatever event they depict.

An *intelligent haunting* is very different. They interact with the living. In fact, this seems to be their purpose. They *want* to make their presence known. Some seem desperate to communicate while others seem to simply want to scare the pants off of you. This type of ghost is generally what people think of when they think of wraiths and specters.

In the following pages you'll meet both kinds, as well as read about some myths and urban legends. You'll meet kindly ghosts and hear about weeping statues in cemeteries, phantom footsteps, disembodied voices, and even the spirit of a famous person or two. Some of the tales included within have been dramatized from accounts told by others. A few even tell of my personal experiences. South Bend and the surrounding area seem to be teeming with spooky tales, full of clanking chains and spectral figures. I've enjoyed learning about these ghosts. I hope you enjoy reading about them.

Chapter One

Tippecanoe Place Restaurant

Located in the heart of South Bend's historic district, Tippecanoe Place promises casual fine dining in an elegant atmosphere. Diners are treated to good food and great service, seated amidst antiques and memorabilia of a day long gone. After dining, the guests are encouraged to take a look around the mansion. They can wander the rooms and gaze at the portraits and the framed photographs on the walls, showing the Studebaker family in their heyday.

They may even catch sight of one of the ghosts of Tippecanoe Place.

The mansion was once the home of Clement Studebaker. Clem arrived in South Bend in 1837 when his father, John Clement Studebaker, moved his wife and ten children to the area and settled in a log cabin south of the city. Clem, then twenty-one years old, went to work for fifty cents a day as a wagon maker.

Courtesy of Tippecanoe Place Restaurant.

Courtesy of Tippecanoe Place Restaurant.

Clem soon married and set up house with his new bride in a single room flat at the corner of Michigan and what is now Western Avenue. Clem and his brother Henry started up their own wagon building and blacksmithing business in 1852, H & C Studebaker. Another of the brothers, John, later bought Henry's share of the business.

When the Civil War commenced in 1861, wagons were in great demand and the business prospered. The Studebakers made thousands of wagons for the Union Army. After the war the westward expansion of the United States kept the brothers busy and prosperous. Many of the families that took the journey across the plains to a new life out west did so in Studebaker wagons. Brother Peter joined the firm, and the Studebaker Brothers Manufacturing Company was born.

After the death of his first wife, Clem remarried in 1864. Second wife Ann Milburn Harper, herself a widow, was the daughter of one of Clem's business associates, George Milburn, who made wagons in nearby Mishawaka. Clem and Ann moved into the William Ruckham house in 1868.

By now the Studebakers were fairly wealthy, and Clem Studebaker, then president of the firm, had many rich and powerful friends. Studebaker now moved in the same circles with the likes of J.P. Morgan, John Wannamaker, and Andrew Carnegie. Clem wanted to build a house that would be more fitting to his wealth and position and where he could host lavish parties. Work on the new mansion, to be known as Tippecanoe Place, was begun in 1886.

Designed by Henry Cobb, the 26,000-square foot mansion had four levels, and boasted forty rooms and twenty fireplaces. It was built by craftsmen using local granite fieldstone for the massive walls. No detail was overlooked. The ornate carvings on the oval doorknobs exemplify the detail that was given to every room of the mansion.

Guests would arrive by carriage at the west entrance. The servants would then show them to the elevator, one of the first in the country, which would take them upstairs where they could freshen up after their journey. They could then make their entrance down the grand staircase where they would meet the other guests in the reception area. Once the dinner gong sounded, they would adjourn to the dining room where a lavish meal awaited them.

The parties were many. In July 1889 son Clem and daughter Ann held a dance party with over fifty people in attendance. The big event, however, was the twenty-fifth wedding anniversary party of Clement and Ann Studebaker. Nearly six hundred guests came on September 13, 1889. They enjoyed the full orchestra that played at the head of the grand staircase, while admiring the new mansion. They were then seated, one hundred at a time, in first level reception, state, and family rooms where eight waiters in full dress served a three-course dinner of the finest delicacies. The party was a huge success and plans were made for the next big event: a reception for members of the Pan-American Congress on October 19.

That party was not to be. A disastrous fire broke out in the early hours of October 9, destroying much of the mansion.

As reported by the *South Bend Times*, a servant, Nellie Bagg, was the first to smell burning wood. Bagg, who shared a room with the nurse girl, Louise Weller, went downstairs to arouse Mrs. Studebaker. Clem was out of town, touring the New England states with members of the Pan-American

Congress. Daughter Ann was in Cincinnati with her brother George and his wife and son Clem was at school in Evanston, leaving an aunt, Isabel Milburn, and Mrs. Studebaker's little grandson as the only other family members in the house.

Mrs. Studebaker traced the smell to a closet by the elevator. Opening the door, she was forced back by the rush of flames. Screaming, the barefoot woman, still in her night attire, raced upstairs to her grandson's room. Mrs.

Tippecanoe Place Restaurant.

Studebaker scooped the small boy in her arms, but found that the flames had spread to the stairs. Panicking, the woman covered the child as best she could with her arms and raced down the stairs. She made it outside, but suffered burns on her neck, shoulders, back, and one side of her face. Mrs. Studebaker's feet and one hand were also severely blistered. The child had a few minor burns.

Portrait of Ann Studebaker, Tippecanoe Place Restaurant.

The servants all made it out, the last being Louise Weller, who, on finding her escape down the stairs impossible, slid down some spouting outside her window. One of the male servants went across the street to the home of L. R. Skerritt, who was Clem Studebaker's private secretary. While they waited for the fire brigade to arrive, Skerritt and several of the servants pulled as many valuable books and pieces of small furniture out of the burning building as they could until smoke and flames made re-entering the house nearly impossible.

A doctor examined Mrs. Studebaker and her grandson and found that while painful, the burns were not severe. The house, however, was not so lucky. By the time the flames were extinguished, the roof was almost entirely gone and several rooms, including Clem Studebaker's bedroom and his beloved den, were utterly destroyed. The rooms that escaped the flames were heavily damaged by smoke and water.

Clem Studebaker, arriving back from the East Coast, immediately set plans in motion to restore the mansion to its former glory, and before long, the Studebakers were once again entertaining their friends at Tippecanoe Place.

A year following the fire, the celebrated Italian artist Signor Luigi Gregori painted a life-size portrait of Mrs. Studebaker and her grandson. The portrait, showing Ann Studebaker rushing down the stairs clutching her grandchild while flames, smoke, and sparks surrounded her, hung on the first landing on the general staircase for many years. Later the painting was willed to Mrs. Studebaker's grandson. It was eventually given to St. Mary's College, which in turn presented it to Notre Dame University. The present whereabouts of the painting are unknown.

The Studebaker business continued to flourish. Clem invested heavily and began to buy up utilities across the country. The family lived happily for years until, like many people, their finances were nearly wiped out by the Stock Market Crash of 1929.

Clem and Ann found they could no longer afford the upkeep on the large mansion. They moved to a nearby apartment, taking with them one maid. Tippecanoe Place became the headquarters for the Red Cross Headquarters, then a school for the handicapped, and, later, a historical museum. It opened as a restaurant on Memorial Day weekend in 1980.

There are two theories as to why Clem Studebaker named his home Tippecanoe Place. One is that the name was in honor of his friend Benjamin Harrison, the 23rd President of the United States. Harrison's grandfather, William Henry Harrison, had been the victor of the battle of Tippecanoe in 1811. Later Harrison, nicknamed "Old Tipp," campaigned for the presidency using the slogan "Tippecanoe and Tyler, Too," the Tyler being his running mate John Tyler. Another theory is that the name came from the fact that the grounds had once been a favorite camping site of Tippecanoe, the chief of the Miami Indians.

It was soon after opening as a restaurant that the ghosts of the past began to make themselves known. One night a manager was closing up alone, as the rest of the staff had already left. He was going through all the rooms, checking that everything was in place and turning off the lights when he suddenly felt he was no longer alone. Nervously, he moved into one of the last rooms and turned to switch off the lights. In the doorway through which he'd just stepped was a woman dressed in white. While the young man could see her features plainly, he could also see *through* her. Frozen in fear, he watched as she walked towards him. Then, as the figure walked *right through him*, the young man felt a mist on his face. He spun around, but the ghostly figure had vanished. Somehow he found the courage to finish closing up for the night, but the next day he called the management team to inform them that he would never again set foot in Tippecanoe Place. He transferred to another restaurant.

14 Tippecanoe Place Restaurant

Stairwell, Tippecanoe Place Restaurant.

Tippecanoe Place Restaurant

Another incident happened on a night that they were taking inventory. Several secretaries and managers were up on the fourth floor checking on the accounts when they were disturbed by a tremendous uproar coming from the attic. It was early in the morning and they knew that no one was up there, but it sounded as if chairs where being thrown about. Worried, they called the police, who arrived with a police dog. By this time the sounds had ceased. The dog was sent up to the attic, but came down in a matter of moments, showing no signs that he had found anything out of order. The police officers then checked out the attic themselves and found nothing amiss. The managers and secretaries were left in the dark as to what had caused the uproar they'd heard.

The bar seems to be a particularly active spot. Bartenders have reported feeling cold spots and seeing "something" just out of the corner of their eyes. The water faucets at the bar often turned on by themselves—workers have said that they've left the room and returned seconds later to find the taps turned fully on, water gushing into the sink. One bartender was serving a drink to a customer who was asking about the ghostly happenings in the restaurant. The bartender had just replied that he didn't believe in ghosts when an expensive bottle of liquor came off the shelf behind him and crashed to the floor!

Lights are often turned back on after an employee has left the room. One Tiffany lamp in particular is often found back on—*even AFTER being unplugged*. The staff usually laugh off these minor occurrences, stating simply, "It's Clem!"

David Barry, the general manager of Tippecanoe Place, has had ghostly experiences of his own. Like others, he's had his troubles with the lights and the water taps in the bar. One night he was closing up the building with a policeman. As they made their way through the rooms, they began to hear a metallic, clanking sound. Barry, used to the sounds of a restaurant after closing, wasn't too worried, thinking that it could be an ice machine making the racket. The sound continued, however, and Barry and the police officer decided to search the mansion to see if they could determine the source. They went through room after room and although they heard the sound several times they could not discover what was making it. Finally they ended up by the back door and they heard the metallic clang once more. It sounded like it came from right behind them. Seeing nothing there, the police officer suggested that they leave. "Whatever is making that sound, a gun isn't going to do any good against it!" the officer insisted.

Courtesy of Tippecanoe Place Restaurant.

Guests have also had ghostly experiences. Some have reported feeling cold spots while others tell of seeing a face behind them in the restroom mirror. Upon turning around, of course, no one is there.

Several paranormal investigations have taken place at the restaurant. One local ghost-hunting group spent the night at the mansion and got some odd energy readings on the third floor by the bar. A Canadian psychic found that the third and fourth floors were particularly active. A television crew from one of the cable networks came out several years ago to tape a segment at the restaurant, but as far as Barry knows it never aired. "I guess we just weren't scary enough," he says with a laugh.

Barry heard a possible explanation for the haunting from the general manager who preceded him. The story goes that one of the Studebakers got one of the maids pregnant. When she came to him, begging him to "make things right," he laughed at her. The despondent maid took her own life that night, hanging herself over the grand staircase.

Whatever the cause, ghosts seem to roam the many rooms of Tippecanoe Place. The diners who come to the restaurant really can't lose. They can be assured of good food and good service served in an elegant atmosphere. And maybe—just maybe—they may encounter one of Tippecanoe Place's specters.

Courtesy of Tippecanoe Place Restaurant.

Primrose Road.

Chapter Two
Are They Haunted—Or Not?

Primrose Road

Anyone who lives in South Bend and is even remotely interested in ghost stories has heard of Primrose Road. The stories and legends surrounding this dark, tree-lined passage are as numerous as the opinions over the veracity of the claims of paranormal activity. Some say it's one of the most haunted sites in the state. Some maintain that it's pure hokum, and that nothing out of the ordinary is found on this road on the northwestern side of the city. Others claim that people seeking ghosts and spirits by driving down this dirt road are in the wrong place entirely—that the haunted Primrose Road is actually located in Potato Creek State Park!

The debate is hotly contested on several Internet sites such as "The Force Forum" and even among ghost hunting groups. If the road is in fact the wrong one, what of the experiences that many claim to have had driving down Primrose Road? Is it a case of the mind expecting something to happen and people reading too much into natural phenomena? Could both roads be haunted? Or is Primrose just a normal road that teenagers have dubbed haunted so they have a fun place to visit on Halloween for a good scare?

Primrose starts off as just another suburban street, but as you drive along, the housing developments, along with the pavement, soon end. Primrose becomes a dirt and gravel road, thickly lined on either side with trees. The foliage is so thick that even in the daylight the area is shrouded in shadows.

The tales are many. One claim is that if you drive down Primrose under twenty miles an hour your tires will be slashed. If you drive over thirty miles an hour, however, the engine will sputter and die and you'll be forced to walk. Maybe a ghostly traffic cop haunts the road and likes to keep vehicles moving at a certain pace. This author and several companions tested this story, but other than providing some opportunities for laughs nothing happened. Perhaps the ghosts watching over vehicle speed were off that night.

If your car does indeed die, don't try calling for help on your cell phone. The area has a way of playing havoc with signals, so even if you manage to get through to someone, your call will be cut off before you can tell the person on the other end of your predicament. You can choose to stay with your car and hope that someone will drive by and assist you, but if you do... you're likely to see eyes staring at you from the surrounding trees. If you brave the road and begin to walk back to civilization, you may encounter a *specter* that will warn you of danger ahead. He'll tell you to go back to your car.

Perhaps you won't run into that unnamed but curiously obliging ghost. You may, however, see the phantom farmhouse. This ramshackle building won't have been visible when you first drove by, but will suddenly appear while you're walking. Sometimes the farmhouse will vanish before you reach it, but on occasion a visitor has actually made it to the door. An old woman will answer a knock on the front door...and if she likes the look of you and invites you in, that is supposed to indicate that you'll be blessed with good luck. If she slams the door in your face, your luck will be extremely bad.

Other claims involve a ghostly red pickup truck. This phantom vehicle seems to be from the 1940s and has been known to chase the unwary that dare to check out the ghostly happenings on Primrose. The truck often vanishes when you look back at it, but will still be visible in your rear view mirror, slowly gaining on you as your foot presses harder on the accelerator.

At one time, according to some sources, a ramshackle shack could be seen through the trees. Anyone daring to get close to this structure would see that the sides of the shack had dozens of dead animals nailed to it.

The clomping of horses' hooves have been reported along the road as well. At times a ghostly stallion will move from one side of the road to the other behind your car.

Other brave souls that have visited this lonely stretch of road have reported that they've felt their hands or arms go entirely numb, and inhuman howls have been heard coming from the swampy lake off to the side of the road. Red lights have been seen to appear at the tops of trees—lights that move in seemingly impossible patterns. One young man said that he had been chased through the woods by a large blue light.

Marcus Foxglove Griffin and his paranormal investigation group WISP (Witches In Search of the Paranormal) went to Primrose Road on September 13, 2005 and had some pretty interesting experiences. Mr. Griffin reports on Ghostvillage.com that, as the group was walking down Primrose, they heard what sounded like a horse snorting. There was no sign of an animal anywhere near them, nor was there any rustling in the foliage to indicate the presence of a horse (or anything else for that matter). Two members of the team found that the power had drained from their cell phones and the same two also felt a very strong urge to leave...*as if something didn't want them there*. As WISP members walked along the road, Mr. Griffin began to hear faint voices. Feeling a paranormal presence, Mr. Griffin and his team began asking questions to see if they could get a response. Using voice recorders, WISP was able to capture some disembodied voices. As an answer to Mr. Griffin's demand that anyone present should show themselves, the recorders picked up what sounds like a child's voice saying, "Can't now." When Mr. Griffin asked, "Can you say that again, please?" another voice answers, saying, "Never!"

The voices and other incidents the group experienced that night left them believing that Primrose Road is VERY haunted indeed.

The stories connected with Primrose Road seem endless. The streetlight at the corner of Brick Avenue and Primrose, for instance, is said to turn on and off at times. There is also Blood Rock, a large stone that was uncovered when workers were clearing out a section of the woods for one of the housing developments. Blood Rock was supposed to have been placed in the middle of a pond at the entrance to the development (or in the front yard of one of the houses, depending on the story being told!) and was said to mysteriously move around. Blood Rock certainly seems to have moved in a rather permanent way. No one I talked with could actually tell me where Blood Rock was. One obliging youth informed me that it had been on the front lawn of a man's house, but that he removed it because he was tired of rubbing off the graffiti that was constantly being painted on it.

The controversy over Primrose Road rages on—with one camp firmly believing that nothing is there; the other insisting that it's one of the most active haunts in South Bend. Interestingly, the listing for Primrose Road on TheShadowlands.net has been removed at the request of property owners in the area. Apparently they are not fond of the reputation and subsequent attention the road has achieved. So if the legends are true and you find yourself stranded on Primrose Road with a car that won't run, don't expect any assistance from the locals. You'd best search for that phantom farmhouse and hope the old woman invites you inside...

†††††††††††††

Adams Street Cemetery

An old graveyard nestled along a country road, Adams Street Cemetery, also known as the Portage Prairie Cemetery, is just as controversial among ghost hunters as Primrose Road. As the cemetery is only about a quarter mile away from the end of Primrose, this is, somehow, fitting. Many people who have traveled up and down Primrose only to waste time and gas have visited Adams Street Cemetery and report having quite a different experience—they report seeing odd mists, strange lights, and floating orbs dancing amongst the gravestones. Others say the old graveyard is just that: a collection of moldering graves with no paranormal activity whatsoever.

Adams Street Cemetery.

One young man, who we'll call Dave, had an unnerving experience in Adams Street Cemetery. Dave, a high school senior at the time, had heard the stories about Primrose and the cemetery and thought that it would be a fun place to take his girlfriend, Shelly. Shelly was apprehensive about visiting any graveyard, let alone a haunted one, in the middle of the night, but Dave had visions of his frightened girlfriend clinging to his arm for protection. They waited until after midnight on a warm September night to start out, and while they drove Dave told Shelly every story he knew about Primrose and Adams Street Cemetery.

Dave drove to about the midpoint of Primrose before pulling off to the side and stopping his engine. He and Shelly got out of the car, but other than the normal sounds of the night they didn't sense anything out of the ordinary happening. After a few minutes they decided to give Adams Street Cemetery a try.

At the cemetery, Shelly stayed by the iron fence, not wanting to move into the graveyard itself. Dave teased her. "Come on. You've got to walk around the tombstones to get the full effect."

"I'm getting enough of an effect from here," she replied, laughing nervously.

Dave, holding their only flashlight, shrugged. "Suit yourself," he said as he began walking away from her. He assumed that she'd soon become frightened enough to join him.

He didn't get far before she let out a stifled scream, stopping him in his tracks. He turned. "What is it?"

He could see her fairly clearly in the moonlight. Her hands were up to her mouth in an almost childlike display of terror. "I saw something."

Dave looked around, letting the beam of his light play along the headstones. "What did you see? Where?"

"A shadow. Over that way." Shelly pointed.

Dave frowned. He couldn't see anything. "It was probably a cat or something."

Shelly shook her head. "That was no cat." Shaking, she turned around. "I'm going back to the car."

Dave sighed as she opened the passenger door and bundled herself inside. "Shelly! Come on! We came out here to see if there was anything to the stories about this place! Don't chicken out just as we're getting started..."

The words trailed away as Dave felt an icy hand grasp his shoulder.

Startled, he quickly turned his head. There was no one behind him. He could still feel the fingers pressing against his sweatshirt. Dave found himself rooted to the spot until he could hear someone exhaling. The sound seemed to be coming from right by his ear, like someone was getting ready to whisper in his ear. The icy hand seemed to push at him, propelling him in the direction of the car.

That was enough for Dave... He vaulted over the iron fence and rushed to the car. Without a word to Shelly, he started the engine and quickly drove away.

That was the LAST time he went ghost hunting.

Chapter Three
Dierdre's Ghost

There was no way that Bailey was going to move from the family home in Peru, Indiana, unless he took his beloved cat, Dierdre, with him. Dierdre had been a major part of Bailey's life since middle school, when Bailey had found the tiny stray hovering around his neighborhood.

Dierdre was a thin white feline with one black patch behind the left ear. From the first day the boy and cat were practically inseparable. Dierdre slept next to Bailey every night. Bailey kept the cat amused with toys and games, often involving yarn that was to be used for his mother's knitting. The two also ate together. Much to his mother's horror, Bailey even went so far as to sometimes share the same plate with the animal. Both being lovers of macaroni and cheese, Bailey would eat some off his plate before lowering it so that Dierdre could have some. After the cat was satisfied, Bailey would finish his meal.

In high school, Bailey rushed home from football practice to spend time with his cat. The attachment Bailey had for Dierdre became a source of gentle ribbing from family and friends. When Bailey began to date, his mother told him laughingly, "You'll never find a girl that you like as much as that cat!"

For his graduation present, Bailey's grandmother arranged for him to take a three week tour through Europe. During his absence, Bailey sent his mother two postcards telling of his travels. Dierdre received four!

It was a forgone conclusion that when Bailey got a job promotion to manage a new video store in South Bend that Dierdre would go with him.

Arrangements had to be made quickly, however, as the new store was opening soon. Bailey quickly located a suitable apartment near downtown and prepared for the move. It wasn't until he actually sat down to sign his new lease that Bailey noticed the 'no pets' clause in the contract. Bailey paused only a moment before signing. He didn't have time to search for a new place, and he figured he could keep Dierdre's presence hidden from the management. After all, she was an indoor cat and possessed a quiet disposition.

The first month went by smoothly. Then a notice was taped to the door informing him that maintenance would be visiting each apartment to change the air filters. The notice caused Bailey some panic. What was to be done with Dierdre?

Luckily an old school friend of Bailey's had also moved to South Bend. Janet lived in a rented house a mere few blocks away and was willing to keep the cat for the day. Dierdre didn't seem to mind being temporarily transplanted, so whenever Bailey needed a hiding place for the animal a trip was made to Janet's place.

This arrangement went on for several years until one Friday afternoon when Dierdre was at Janet's due to a pest control visit at the apartment complex. Janet usually let the cat have the run of the house, especially if she had to work that day or was out shopping. Unfortunately this time Janet had forgotten that one of the kitchen windows was slightly open. It was enough room for Dierdre, who must have been in the mood to explore, to squeeze through and make her escape.

When Janet came home to find her friend's pet missing, she frantically searched the house and yard. Finally realizing the cat had wandered too far, she knew that she had to inform Bailey. She dreaded making the call, but knew it had to be done.

Bailey raced over and he and Janet continued the search. Soon they enlisted the aid of several friends and co-workers. Over a dozen people combed the neighborhood, but no trace of Dierdre could be found.

That night a despondent Bailey slept alone in his bed. The next day he arranged the schedule so he could be off for a few days so he could continue to look for Dierdre. He searched everywhere and put up fliers with Dierdre's picture and an offer of a reward on every telephone pole. His cell phone rang several times, but it was always a friend asking if the cat had been found yet. No one, it seemed, had seen Dierdre.

That Saturday night Bailey came home from work fairly late. As he started to undress for bed, he heard a sound coming from outside his bedroom window. His heart began to beat faster. It was a cat's meow and, although the noise was faint, Bailey was sure it was Dierdre. He looked out of the window, but could see no cat. The mewling grew louder, though, and now Bailey was sure it came from his beloved Dierdre.

Bailey raced outside and cried out in joy when he saw the thin white cat pacing up and down the sidewalk. There was even the black patch behind the left ear, leaving no doubt that the animal was indeed Dierdre. As Bailey rushed forward to scoop the animal into his arms, the cat looked up at him, recognition in her eyes.

When Bailey got close, however, the cat darted forward. Bailey ran to catch up, but no matter how fast he went, the cat remained out of his reach. It struck Bailey as odd that the cat seemed to move without making any sounds. She also didn't seem to change her pace, but yet she always remained out of Bailey's grasp. It was a dark night so Bailey couldn't be sure, but it also seemed like Dierdre's paws *weren't* actually touching the pavement. Following the cat, Bailey began to fear that he wasn't in the presence of a living animal. He slowed down, tears stinging his eyes, wondering where Dierdre was leading him.

It was well after midnight and few people were walking the streets so Bailey had no chance to ask a passing stranger if they could see the cat as well. Some cars went past them, but other than that Bailey was alone with the phantom feline. He trailed along behind Dierdre for several blocks until finally the cat paused and looked back at him one last time. Then she took a few steps towards some bushes and...*vanished* into thin air.

Bailey knew before he looked what he would find behind the bushes. He approached quietly, since the bushes where on private property and it would be hard to explain why he was slinking around someone's yard in the middle of the night.

Dierdre's body was indeed hidden behind the bushes. From her injuries Bailey concluded that the cat had been clipped by a car's tire and had gone behind the bush to die. With tears streaming down his face, Bailey picked her up and carried her home.

He found a wooden box to put her in and the next day drove back to his parents' house in Peru to bury her behind the garage. Bailey even carved a wooden cross with Dierdre's name on it to use as a headstone.

Today Bailey has two cats and lives with his girlfriend in Mishawaka, but Dierdre will always have a special place in his heart. When he recounts his story, Bailey says, "I'm not sure what people find more unbelievable, the fact that I think my cat's ghost led me to her body or that I made a headstone for her!"

Chapter Four

The Gipper & Notre Dame's Ghosts

The Ghosts of Washington Hall

It was a cool, crisp night in 1925. Pio Montenegro, a student from Brazil, took a break from his homework and wandered over to the window. Gazing out, Pio frowned as a strange white shape seemed to be approaching Washington Hall. Pressing his face against the glass, Pio could make out a figure on a white horse. He watched in amazement as the pale figure steered his charger straight up the front steps. Horse and rider promptly *vanished*, but not before Pio got a good look at the face of the man. It was none other than George Gipp, Notre Dame football legend.

George Gipp had died of pneumonia five years previously, and Pio Montenegro was the first person to catch sight of Washington Hall's most famous spirit.

He was not the last.

George Gipp, born February 18, 1895, came from Laurium, a small town in Michigan's Upper Peninsula. As a child Gipp showed little sports prowess and seemed even less interested in academics. It wasn't until high school that Gipp discovered baseball. He often played on a local field with his friends, and it was on the diamond that Gipp found he had a natural talent for the game. Gipp joined the Laurium baseball team, where he played center field. Gipp became an all-around athlete, also participating in track, hockey, and sandlot football.

His schoolwork still suffered, and Gipp's disinterest in academics led the young man to ditch class at any opportunity. The high school principal later claimed that Gipp was in his office at least monthly for disciplinary action.

There is some question as to whether Gipp ever officially graduated high school. In either case, Gipp had no plans to go to college. He wasn't that fond of study, and he also had little money.

It was in the summer of 1916 that one of his old friends, Wilbur Gray, suggested to Gipp that he try out for a baseball scholarship so that he could attend Notre Dame. Gray was a semiprofessional player in Elkhart, Indiana, and was impressed with Gipp. Gipp was dubious at first, but his friend persisted and he finally agreed to give it a try.

Before long, George Gipp was enrolled as a freshman at Notre Dame. Gipp found it difficult to fit in with his classmates. He was older than most of the other freshmen, and finances were a constant problem. Gipp soon fell back into his old habits and began skipping classes. Several times he almost gave up and packed his bags to return home. Baseball was the only thing keeping Gipp at Notre Dame. He loved the game and dreamed of eventually joining the Chicago Cubs as their centerfield.

Things changed for Gipp when he and a friend were out kicking a football around. Off to the side, a stocky man smoking a cigar watched carefully. When Gipp came close to retrieve the ball, the man introduced himself as Knute Rockne. Rockne asked Gipp if he'd played football in high school. Gipp replied that he had little interest in football. Baseball was his game. Rockne suggested that Gipp should attend football practice the following day. Gipp agreed, and before long the boy from Laurium was a starter on the Notre Dame football team.

Gipp quickly became Rockne's star player. While his official Hall of Fame listing shows his position as halfback, Rockne found he could use Gipp in nearly any position. During his tenure at Notre Dame, the Gipper, as he was now known, amassed 4,100 total yards in rushing and passing and another 4,100 plus yards in punts and kickoffs. He also scored more than 150 points. While playing defensive back, Gipp never allowed a completed pass.

Off the field, Gipp was getting a reputation as a gambler. Gipp was fond of cards and began making large bets on craps, poker games, and even billiards. Gipp's favorite places to gamble were Hullie's, Mike's Pool Parlor, and the Oliver Hotel. He was even known to place bets on Notre Dame football games. According to the official website for George Gipp, Rockne was admonishing the team during halftime of the 1920 Army game. Gipp seemed uninterested in his coach's words, taking a drag off a cigarette that a teammate had lit up. Irate, Rockne asked Gipp if he was at all interested in the game. With a slight smile, Gipp replied, "Look, Rock, I've got $400 bet on this game and I'm not about to blow it."

Gipp was expelled for a short period in 1919. According to some sources, Gipp was expelled for cutting classes, but others maintain that Gipp had been discovered exiting a notorious South Bend dance hall that was strictly off limits to Notre Dame students. Whatever the reason, football fans responded quickly and made their displeasure known. Local hardware stores reported record sales of tar and feathers! Rockne panicked, since as soon as word got out, rival coaches began to try to recruit Gipp. To make sure he would be heard, Rockne got several prominent South Bend residents to back him and soon the entire town was clamoring to get Gipp back. The administration office got the point and reinstated Gipp, who was back on the football field in days.

To Gipp's credit, he was generous with his gambling winnings. He was known to give food money to impoverished families in South Bend. Several times he helped out friends who found themselves short of tuition fees.

The Gipper's gambling often kept him out late, which may have led to his ultimate demise. Many times Gipp returned to the campus late, only to find himself locked out of his dorm room. Gipp's dormitory was overseen by Brother Marilius, who was not overly fond of Notre Dame's star football player. Marilius felt Gipp was too brash and cocky, and was displeased that the football player often stayed out late for parties and gambling. The two men clashed often, but one thing became clear—Marilius would no longer put up with Gipp's late arrivals to the dorm. If Gipp couldn't make his curfew, Marilius would initiate disciplinary action. If he did, Gipp's football career could be in jeopardy. Rather than face Marilius on those late nights, Gipp found other accommodations.

According to several reports, Gipp often crept into Washington Hall, which was Notre Dame's performing arts center, to sleep. Gipp was a steward for the building and knew that the back door was often left unlocked. If the back door to Washington Hall was locked, Gipp would then sleep on the steps leading up to the front entrance.

Was it one of these nights sleeping on the cold stone steps of Washington Hall that led to the bout of pneumonia that would bring an end to Notre Dame's first All-American?

During the 1920 game against Indiana, Gipp suffered a slight shoulder injury. This kept him on the bench for most of the following week's game against Northwestern. Rockne, finally acquiescing to the pleas of both Gipp and the crowd, allowed his star player out onto the field during the last quarter. Gipp threw a fifty-five-yard pass to Norman Barry that resulted in a touchdown. It was the last pass the Gipper would ever throw.

After the Northwestern game, Gipp found himself with a bad strep throat infection. This soon turned to pneumonia and on November 23, Gipp was admitted to St. Joseph's Hospital.

Despite the best efforts of his doctors, Gipp's condition continued to deteriorate. Newspaper and radio reporters waited breathlessly in the hospital's lobby, anxious for any word. Finally, on December 12, the doctors summoned Gipp's family and Coach Rockne. The Gipper was dying. Gipp weakly motioned for his coach to come closer and spoke those immortal words, "I've got to go, Rock. It's all right. I'm not afraid. Some time, Rock, when things are wrong and the breaks are beating the boys—tell them to go in there with all they've got and win just one for the Gipper. I don't know where I'll be then, Rock. But I'll know about it, and I'll be happy."

The story of Gipp's stirring speech may be apocryphal. Rockne was well known as a stirring speechmaker and knew just what to say to move his audience. It wasn't until eight years later that Rockne revealed the Gipper's plea, and that was to rally his team during a game against Army that was going badly. If George Gipp never uttered that speech, it at least made for a thrilling moment in the film Knute Rockne, All American, which featured a young Ronald Reagan as the Gipper. Reagan had wanted the role badly, and even used the slogan "Win One For The Gipper" during his presidential campaign years later.

George Gipp hung on for a few more days, but passed away on December 14, 1920.

On December 17, the train bearing Gipp's casket pulled out of South Bend, heading to Calumet, Michigan, where the football legend was to be buried. As reported by Mark Marimen in his book *Haunted Indiana,* nearly the entire student body and many residents of South Bend turned out to convey their respects.

If the stories are to be believed, though, George Gipp's spirit returned to watch over the campus he loved. Since then, the Gipper has often been seen riding a horse up the steps leading to the front entrance to Washington Hall. Footsteps have been heard walking down the hallways. Doors have mysteriously opened or closed. Students have found that personal objects often disappear only to be found several days later.

While the ghost has been fairly quiet in recent years, he still has shown up from time to time. As reported in the *ND Observer Online*, one of the nighttime custodial staff may have had a run in with the Gipper.

Roger Allee was working by himself in one of the halls. As he watched, a shadow, seemingly of a man, appeared on the wall near him. Allee looked around to ensure that he was alone. No one else was in the hall. Looking back at the shadow, Allee was shocked to see that the shape was getting bigger. The shoulders of the figure were padded, like he was wearing football gear.

Washington Hall's Other Specters

The ghost of George Gipp is not the only specter to walk the corridors of Washington Hall. In July of 2000, Allee was in the worker's break room, located in the backstage area of the Hall, when he suddenly felt a presence. Allee looked around the doorway and saw a transparent figure standing there. It was an older man, who looked at Allee with a wide grin before promptly vanishing.

Washington Hall has had visits from several musical ghosts as well. One spirit may be that of Jim Minaui, a student professor and trumpet player who died in his room in 1919. The following year Joe Cassanta, a resident of the hall, was awakened around 3 a.m. by the sound of a trumpet. Cassanta sat up in his bed and then heard the sound of feet pattering on the floor right next to his bed.

The trumpet playing ghost soon became very active, awakening students on a nearly nightly basis. Some students would wake up and sit up in fear, too petrified to even alert their roommates.

While at times the spirits that inhabit Washington Hall may seem mischievous or playful, they have also been known at times to be helpful. In the late 1970s, some theater students decided to stage a late-night session with an Ouija board to contact the ghosts. The building stopped being used for student housing back in the 1950s and was generally locked by eleven o'clock, so one student had to hide among the shadows of the catwalks while the Hall was being locked up for the night. Once he was sure the coast was clear, he crept down to allow his fellow thespians inside. They made their way to the center of the stage and set up their Ouija board. They lit candles to illuminate the area. With fingers touching the planchette, they asked if there were any spirits that wanted to speak to them. Slowly the planchette moved first to the letter S and then to the letter G. After a short pause, the pointer suddenly shot over to the area of the board where GOODBYE was written. Puzzled by this answer, the students asked the question a second time. Once again the planchette moved to the S and then to the G, sliding finally to the GOODBYE once again. The students decided to call it a night and packed up their things.

They left the building and gathered in the parking lot, talking about their experience. Looking back at Washington Hall, they saw a light flashing behind the door they had just exited. Quickly, they hid behind some nearby bushes. The door burst open to reveal a security guard. He'd been making his rounds and had nearly caught the students performing their aborted séance. The students were sure that the spirits were sending them a warning and that S. G. stood for Security Guard.

Of late the ghosts of Washington Hall have been relatively quiet. There are still the odd sounds and the creak of a floorboard here and there, but these can be attributed to the age of the building. Still, there are times when students feel like they're being watched. They turn quickly only to find no one there. Maybe the spirits aren't as dormant as some believe.

††††††††††††††

The Spirits of St. Mary's College

"Can I Have My Things Back?"

Legend has it that the ghost of a young girl has often been seen hanging from the bell tower of Le Mans Hall. The girl, despondent and desperate, took her own life ages ago, but seems to be unable to completely vanish from the area where her final act took place.

Le Mans Hall is one of the dormitories at St. Mary's College, located at Notre Dame. St. Mary's was founded in 1844 by the Sisters of the Holy Cross as a private Catholic liberal arts college. The college has long been known for its excellence, and has in fact been picked as the #1 college in its category in the *U.S. News* and *World Report* annual survey twelve times in the last thirteen years. It is one of the oldest institutions in the country providing higher education for women.

Ghost stories have always been a part of Le Mans Hall. The oral tradition of passing the legends on to new students has been encouraged. The ghosts that roam its halls are as much a part of Le Mans and St. Mary's as the books and classrooms. Looking at Le Mans Hall, it's easy to believe the place could be haunted. The six-story central bell tower looms over the four-story dormitory like a protective force.

The bell tower ghost is hardly the only specter that haunts the dormitory. Over the years students have been plagued by strange footsteps echoing down the corridors, toilets repeatedly flushing on their own, bangs in the wall, and even the ringing of unplugged telephones. Shadowy figures emerge from walls and even posters. One of Le Mans' Resident Assistants has repeatedly seen a strange blob floating down the hall between rooms 273 and 274.

Personal items often go missing from rooms. Shoes, items of clothing, and jewelry will often disappear, only to be found a day or two later. Once a toothbrush vanished from a student's bathroom, only to be found in her desk drawer. Her friends proclaimed their innocence. It was just another prank played by the spirits of Le Mans.

Some students say that if you find an item missing, you should immediately look around the room and ask, "Can I have my things back?" The ghosts will then return whatever they took—although you may have to search a bit. A broach that had last been seen on top of a dresser may turn up inside a shoe in the closet.

Some have also seen a male ghost, usually around room 401, who may be the cause of the banging on the walls. He appears to be a gruff man wearing overalls and is reputed to be a farmer whose grave was relocated when Holy Cross Hall was built in 1903. The hammering on the walls may indeed be him, since maintenance workers have checked the pipes and searched for rats or mice and can find nothing to account for the sounds.

The hallway known as Queen's Court has its own ghost, whom the students have named Mary. Mary has often been seen as a shadowy figure that quickly vanishes, although she more often makes her presence known by her echoing footsteps. Mary is supposed to be the spirit of a girl who took her own life in one of the rooms at the end of the hall.

There are also rumors that a stillborn baby was left in the bathroom of Queen's Court. On still nights, students have heard a baby's cry.

Tales are also told of the Woman in the Red Cape. She is seen mainly in the chapel, where she goes around extinguishing candles.

Behind Regina Hall is a graveyard, usually reserved for nuns. Buried under a large monument, however, is a student named Zellie Selby. Zellie died in 1870 after a sudden illness. Her father was a traveling judge in Tennessee with no established residence, so Zellie was interred at St. Mary's. It is said that Zellie watches over the campus and that her silhouette can be seen etched into the base of the monument.

Another tale concerns Lake Marian, an artificial lake near Le Mans Hall. When workmen were building the lake in the early 1900s, they discovered a woman buried in a shallow grave. According to legend, they opted not to move her and she's still buried at the end of the lake. If you look down into the waters, sometimes you can see her face staring back up at you.

There seems to be a plethora of ghosts roaming St. Mary's, but the students don't seem to mind. In fact, they speak of their otherworldly visitors with pride. The ghosts are part of what makes St. Mary's such a special place.

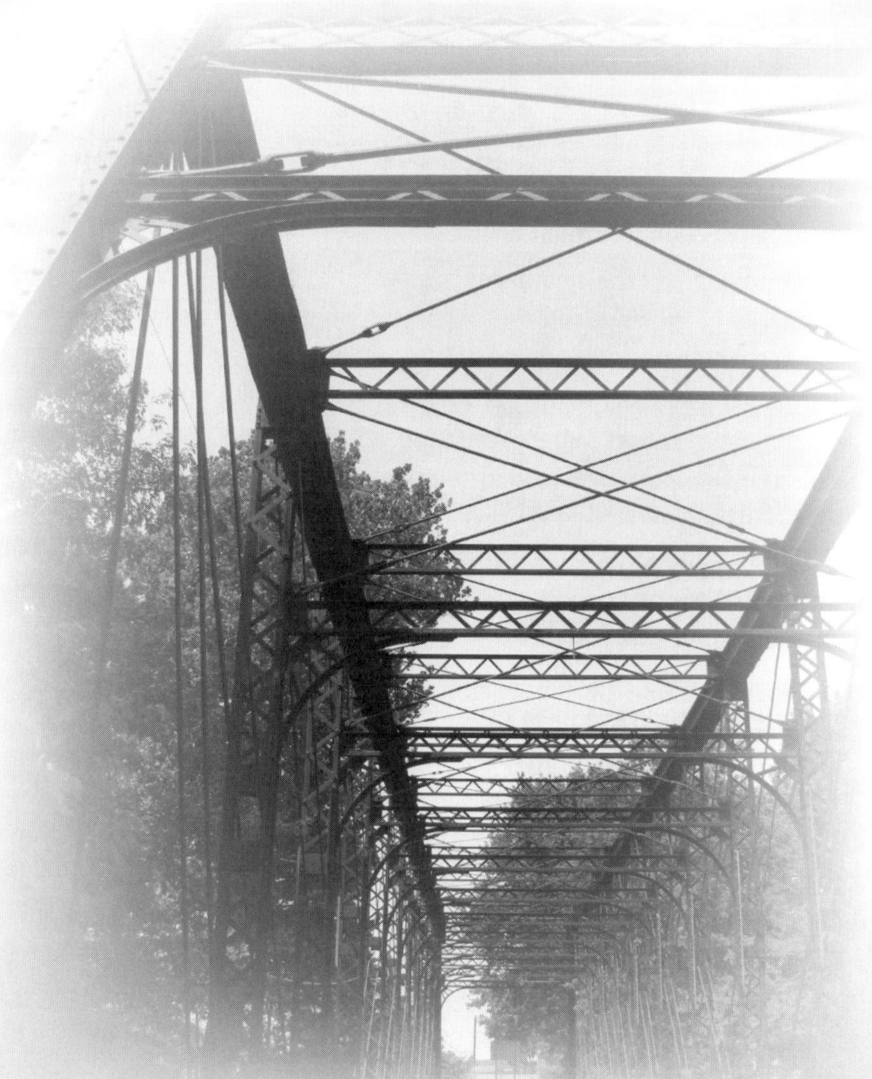

Chapter Five
On the Trail of Ghosts

My Night With South Bend Paranormal Task Force

Dogface Bridge

It was nearly a dark and stormy night.

My friend Frank and I met the folks from South Bend Paranormal Task Force, a group of family and friends who are also ghost hunters, at a steak restaurant early on a Saturday evening. Jill Sweeney, leader and founder of the group, arrived with members Teddy, Maclin, and Andrew. Another member, Michael, known to one and all as Dashner, would be joining us later in the evening. All evening the skies sputtered with rain and dark clouds hovered overhead. Frank and I, not knowing where the investigation was to take place, began to worry that we hadn't dressed warmly enough for a cold, wet night out.

While enjoying our dinner, Jill informed us that our first trip would be to a place known as Dogface Bridge. After that, she suggested that we venture to Oak Ridge Cemetery in Goshen. The cemetery had previously been very successful for the group and they were anxious to revisit the site. Never having been on a ghost hunt before, I wasn't sure how I'd cope if anything particularly scary occurred. Across the table from me was Andrew, the smallest member of the group. Andrew somewhat resembled a young Harry Potter, so I decided that if anything jumped out at us I would throw him in its path while I made a hasty retreat. Andrew wouldn't be able to stop anything, but perhaps he could slow down whatever it was long enough for me to make my escape.

We swapped ghost stories until we had finished eating and then went to pick up the remaining team member. By the time we set out, the rain had stopped and the air warmed considerably. We drove into the countryside, twisting and turning through a seemingly endless series of rural roads. Jill's GPS system seemed determined to keep us from our final destination. More than once we had to backtrack and find a turn that had been missed. Finally we found the gravel road that would take us to...Dogface Bridge.

During our drive, Maclin had told us the story of the now demolished bridge. Apparently, some years ago a young couple was driving over the bridge when a dog suddenly appeared in their headlights. The young man swerved to avoid hitting the animal, sending the vehicle over the side of the bridge. The car plunged into the icy water below and the couple drowned. Legends now tell of people seeing phantom hounds in the vicinity or of hearing the squeal of tires when no car is present. Often the young woman passenger is seen standing by the ruins of the bridge. At times her face is obscured entirely, but sometimes she is seen to have the face of a dog, thus giving the bridge its present name.

The gravel road came to an end so we parked our vehicles and the ghost hunters got their equipment ready. Armed with digital cameras, voice recorders, and an EMF detector, the team explained that to get to the actual site we'd have to get across another bridge and traverse a large section of woods. The first bridge was an old, wooden structure, which, at first, seemed to be in fairly good shape. Unfortunately, at the far end, a good four-foot section of the wooden planks were missing entirely, leaving a gaping hole. The iron supports were still in place, however, so with no difficulty we got across.

As I carefully crossed the gap, I tried not to think about what Maclin had told us back in the car. On a previous investigation, the team had been crossing this bridge when suddenly they'd heard a loud rapping on the underside of the bridge. They could find no explanation for the sound. Perhaps something had been telling them not to proceed...

The night was clear and still, but once we entered the woods the canopy of trees cut off the light from the stars so we had to use flashlights to keep from falling over logs and branches. We followed a path that had at one time obviously been a road. We seemed to walk for ages, climbing over fallen trees and avoiding large pits in the road. As we got closer to our destination, we could hear dogs barking. A light far off through the woods told us that someone lived close enough that our flashlights were alarming their animals, so we switched them off whenever we could. Finally we came to the end of the woods. In front of us was a creek and what had, at one time, been a bridge. Little of it now remained. Jill brought out her digital voice recorder and attempted to get some EVPs *(Electronic Voice Phenomena—voices that are captured on tape that aren't heard at the time)* while Dashner snapped pictures with the digital camera.

Nothing unusual was showing up in his photos, and none of us were getting the feeling that anything uncanny was happening around us.

Peering across the water, Jill noticed that a car was parked opposite us where the other end of the bridge had once been. Whoever it was didn't seem disturbed by our presence, however, as they remained silent. I wondered if perhaps the car had been abandoned, but Jill thought she saw someone walking in front of the car occasionally. Feeling that Dogface Bridge was letting us down in terms of paranormal activity that night, we decided to make our way back to our cars. Unless something showed up later on the voice recorders, the woman with the dog's face had seemingly taken the night off.

We began to load the equipment back into the vehicles when someone noticed headlights coming down the gravel road towards us. To be more precise, one headlight, since one was apparently out. We watched as a beat-up pickup truck pulled in behind our cars and two rather inebriated young men got out.

"You guys checking out Dogface Bridge?" the driver asked, his words slurring. The spirits of Dogface Bridge weren't the only ones he'd encountered over the evening, obviously. Jill informed him that we had indeed been checking out the area, but that we now wanted to leave and his truck was blocking our path. After some persuasion he and his companion got back into their vehicle. He sped off down the gravel road rather quickly—too quickly. At one point the driver nearly lost control of the truck and they came close to careening off into a ditch.

We may not have found ghosts at Dogface Bridge, but we nearly witnessed an accident that could have resulted in more spirits haunting the area.

Oakridge Cemetery

After leaving Dogface Bridge, we began a long trek to Goshen to visit Oakridge Cemetery. During the drive we exchanged favorite quotes from Monty Python and Mel Brooks' movies to pass the time, an activity that started when Frank and I quoted our favorite line from "Young Frankenstein" — "Could be worse...Could be raining!" Arriving in Goshen, we stopped for refreshments at a gas station. The girl working the register asked us where we were from, as she was obviously wondering what we were doing in her small town. She informed me that the only things to be found in Goshen were "drunk teenagers and Amish buggies." I hoped she was incorrect and that some paranormal activity could be found there as well.

We found the cemetery a few blocks away. Jill had informed the sheriff's department of our investigation prior to our arrival, so we found the entrance and drove straight inside.

Oakridge Cemetery is famous for the statue that stands over the grave of Michael Bashor. The statue of a male angel towers over the grave, atop a marble monument. According to legend, at times the angel weeps tears of blood. I had searched the Internet for any record as to why this story has persisted, but could find no explanation for the legend. Bashor had been one of the founders of Bashor's Childrens Home, but there was no tale of tragedy that seemed to be connected with him.

On Ghostvillage.com I did find a report from Marcus Foxglove Griffin, who had interviewed an unnamed man who lived across from the cemetery. The neighbor reported that people often visited the cemetery at night, but that for the most part they didn't cause any disturbance and that he

Angel statue in Oakridge Cemetery.

rarely had to call the police. The man had, however, seen some things he couldn't explain. On three separate occasions he'd seen a woman dressed in a white dress walk slowly through the cemetery. She would stop in front of Michael Bashor's grave and lower her head, and the sound of her crying would be carried on the wind. Then, as the man watched, she'd suddenly vanish. At other times the man would see shadows moving amongst the headstones.

On a previous visit to Goshen, the SBPTF team had been using their digital recorders to try to catch some EVPs. Listening to the tapes afterwards, Dashner had heard a voice saying, in a rather sinister whisper, "You're cursed!" He didn't put a lot of stock in it, but several days later he dislocated his foot at football practice when the trainer stepped on it. Dashner, for one, was uneasy being back at Oakridge Cemetery.

Finding the monument was easy even in the large graveyard, as the monument is at least fifteen feet tall. We left our cars and walked slowly to the grave. The SBPTF team took digital photographs along the way, hoping to find some anomalies. Lots of pictures of Michael Bashor's grave were taken, and we read the inscription in the marble. Bashor had lived for seventy-four years, six months, and nine days. Judging by the symbol adorning his stone, he'd been a freemason. It was easy to see how the legend of the angel crying tears of blood came about. The years had stained and eroded the angel's face. A reddish-brown mark covered most of the angel's right cheek. The left side of the angel's face bore several stains directly under the eye. In the darkness of the night, the stains could indeed look like blood.

I had my voice recorder on as we left Bashor's grave to check out other areas of the cemetery. As we walked around, it seemed to me that I could see something moving between two trees ahead of us. Whatever it was, it moved extremely quickly. I waited to see if anyone else spotted it. Jill, leading the way, stopped suddenly. She played her flashlight beam towards the trees I'd been watching and asked if anyone else had seen something moving. Several of us had.

We immediately went to check out the area, but could find no sign of whatever it was we'd seen. No one could have moved away from the spot without us seeing them. I recalled the report from the neighbor, who'd seen things moving around the cemetery. *Was something paranormal making itself known to us?*

We moved to another area, which Jill informed us contained many children's graves. There had been reports of weird sounds in this part of the cemetery, such as footsteps following you or even coming towards you when no one was around. Loud thuds had also been heard, as if something had fallen out of the trees. The team continued to take pictures, finding several orbs showing up in their photos. Battery drain became an issue, despite the fact that new batteries had been placed in the cameras prior to setting out. Other members of the team used digital voice recorders in hopes of catching EVPs. The *orbs*, which are floating balls of energy and light, were photographed by one tree in particular.

It was late and we were getting tired, so we decided to call it a night. Frank and I planned to drive straight home, so we said our farewells and began the long trek home.

Several days later I was listening to my voice recorder; I used it mostly for interviews, but had left it on at various times that night. I listened again to the conversation we'd been having as we strolled away from the grave of Michael Bashor. Jill and Dashner were discussing their previous trip to Oakridge. During a pause in the conversation I could hear what sounded like a whisper. "Get out." I replayed the tape several times. Sure enough, there was a voice I couldn't identify telling us to **get out**! The voice had to have been close to the microphone, and the recorder had been in my hand at the time. I certainly didn't hear anything at the time.

Maybe we hadn''t been alone at Oakridge Cemetery after all...

Chapter Six
Grandmother's House

Tony's grandmother's house is no longer there, having been torn down to make way for a new medical clinic. Granny herself died years before that, and the house remained empty until it was demolished. Tony, however, remembers the house very well. It's almost as if he can still see the two story brick dwelling, built sometime in the 1930s. He and his brother, Rick, spent many days there as children, since Granny babysat while Tony's parents worked.

Tony generally enjoyed the times spent at his Grandmother's. She kept lots of toys and games handy to entertain the two boys, along with nearly every Dr. Seuss book ever written. The house, having lots of rooms, was also good for games of Hide and Go Seek. There was a basement, which had held the washing machine and dryer, and an attic. One of the upstairs rooms had been changed over from a sewing room to the children's playroom. The basement was usually off-limits to the kids. The stairs were old and not in the best of repair and Granny worried that the boys might get hurt down there. Tony was fine with this. The basement was a little on the dark and creepy side, seemingly full of spiders and shadowy areas where anything might be lurking.

It was in the basement that Tony had his first experience. His grandmother, tired from a full day of gardening and housework, asked him to go down and bring up the last load of laundry for folding. "Be careful on those steps, mind you," she warned him. "Make sure you use the handrail."

Tony, who was eleven at the time and small for his age, crept down the stairs with extreme caution. He was certain that a skeletal hand was going to shoot between the steps and grab him by the ankles at any moment. Finally he reached the last step with no incident. Feeling braver, he strode over to the dryer and tossed the still-warm clothing into a laundry basket. The load was heavy for a small boy and he knew he wouldn't be able to hold on to the handrail on his way back up the stairs. Hadn't Granny thought of that? Well, he'd just have to go even slower...and if he needed to drop the basket and run the rest of the way up the steps, then he would. Surely safety was more important than a stupid load of clean clothes.

Tony had made it about halfway up the stairs when he heard a door close behind him. He froze, grasping the laundry basket tightly. He knew that there was no one in the basement. He'd have seen them. Besides, there was just Granny and Rick in the house, and he knew Granny was up in the living room watching television and Rick was up in the playroom.

Then he heard someone laugh. It was a deep, guttural sound unlike anything Tony had ever heard before. Hardly daring to breathe, Tony bolted up the remaining steps, somehow managing to keep hold of the laundry basket. Reaching the top, he slammed the basement door behind him. Nothing would entice him to journey back down there by himself.

Today, Tony realizes the shutting door he heard could have been one of several cupboards or closets that were down in the basement. The opening of the basement door *could* have created enough of a draft to cause a door to swing shut. The chuckling sound, though, is something he still can't dismiss. It wasn't the water or heat pipes. He was used to those sounds. This sound was definitely human...or *inhuman*.

Tony didn't tell Rick about his experience. He knew his older brother would just laugh and make fun of him. He simply informed his grandmother that the basement was a creepy place he would rather not visit again. Granny nodded sagely. "It *is* dark and damp down there. Certainly not the place for a little boy." Tony was glad when the next time a trip down to the basement was called for that Granny asked Rick to go.

Nothing else happened for quite some time. Rick and Tony spent most of their days up in the playroom, going through the books and making up their own rules for the many board games that Granny bought for them. Most of the furniture had been pulled out of the playroom, so they had plenty of space to set up racetracks or whatever they wanted. One door in the playroom led to the attic, but this was generally kept shut. After all, there were only dusty old boxes kept in there. Rick and Tony had, on an adventurous day, explored the attic, but had found little to interest young boys. Rick had been interested in their grandfather's old trunk, which had his uniform from World War II and some other memorabilia, but that hadn't excited Tony. Why should a bunch of clothes and papers of a man he'd never met interest him? He had coaxed Rick back to the playroom, where board games awaited.

One day they had been playing when Rick paused. "You know that the attic is haunted, don't you?"

Tony frowned. He remembered the sounds he'd heard down in the basement and while he'd never heard anything unusual coming from the attic, it wasn't impossible that a ghost would reside there. Still, he figured Rick was trying to scare him, so he replied, "No, it isn't."

"Sure it is."

"Who is it haunted by?"

Rick shrugged. "Some lady. She must have owned this house years ago. She lives in the attic and comes out to scare little boys."

Now Tony knew he was being teased. "Yeah, right."

"No, it's true. I bet you're *too scared* to go in there by yourself."

Tony assured his brother that he wasn't. They got up and walked over to the attic door. "You've got to spend five minutes in there," Rick challenged.

Tony agreed as they opened the door.

The room was lit by a single bare bulb and, though it didn't provide a lot of light, it did manage to throw monstrous shadows against the walls. Rick insisted the ghost wouldn't come out if the light was on, however, so Tony was shut into the room with his only light source being the small, grimy window at the far end of the attic.

Tony sat down on one of the chairs that had been removed from the playroom. He didn't feel that anything scary was in the room with him, so all he had to do was wait out his five minutes.

He looked around and for a moment thought he saw a woman standing in the corner. His heart began to beat faster until he realized it was a tailor's dummy, a remnant from when the playroom had been a sewing room. That, he supposed, had been Rick's ghost. He was supposed to have seen that and freak out. Rick would be disappointed when Tony emerged from the attic room.

Not getting the response he had hoped, Rick began to scratch at the attic door, which only made Tony smile to himself. When the five minutes had elapsed, Tony emerged. Rick, bearing his most serious face, asked, "Didn't you hear the scratching?"

"Yeah, I did. That was you."

Rick, of course, insisted that it wasn't, but Tony knew better. The attic wasn't haunted at all. Tony was glad he'd never told his brother about what had happened down in the basement. Tony knew that he wouldn't last five minutes alone down there! Finally Rick tired of the game and let Tony out. Just as Tony began to step out of the attic it seemed as if a cold breeze hit him. It was a momentary sensation, one that didn't mean anything to Tony at the time. It was only later in life when Tony heard about cold spots occurring in haunted places that the scene came back to him with added clarity.

As it turned out, Rick had been right about a ghost being in the house, but it wasn't a female nor did it have anything to do with the attic room.

Weeks later, Tony emerged from the playroom to go down to the kitchen for a drink. Across from the playroom was a spare bedroom, which was normally shut up since it was rarely used. This day, though, the door to this room was wide open. Tony, being naturally curious, peeked inside.

A tall, thin man was seated on the bed. He was wearing a military uniform and seemed to be in great distress. His shoulders sagged and he had his hands to his face. Tony gasped, wondering whom Granny had let into the house. The man seemed to hear the sound for he looked up and smiled weakly at the boy...*then he vanished as if he'd never been there at all*.

This time Tony rushed to tell his brother what he'd seen. Rick, knowing ghosts had been on their minds since the attic challenge, scoffed. "You imagined it," he insisted. "There wasn't any man there." To prove his point, he pulled his younger brother back into the spare bedroom. "See? Nothing here."

There was, and Tony pointed out an indentation in the bed where the man had sat. Rick was not impressed, however. Granny, upon being told, was more sympathetic. She told Rick that odd things sometimes happen. "I've *seen* things myself," she said. "So you never know."

She sat Tony down on the couch and pulled out an old photo album. Finding the page she wanted, she pointed to a certain photograph of a young couple. The photo was old and faded, but Tony instantly recognized the man. "That's him! That's the man I saw."

Granny smiled. She pointed to the woman in the portrait. "That was me, many years ago. And that," she said, indicating the man in the worn photo, "was your grandfather."

Chapter Seven
Sister of Mercy

Not all ghosts are scary wraiths intent on frightening the unwary. Ghosts can be playful, sad, and happy...and, at least in the case of the spectral nun who used to roam the halls of St. Joseph Community Hospital, caring.

St. Joseph is a small hospital, one that has a reputation for personal and top-notch medical care often not found in hospitals in larger cities. The story of how St. Joseph came to be actually starts back in the mid-1800s in Germany. Katherine Kasper, like most of the people who lived in the tiny village of Dernbach, was poor. Kasper, however, was passionate about helping out her friends and neighbors in any way possible. She began to look after the sick, doing whatever she could to ease their suffering. She often kept watch over the dying, giving them company in their last hours on earth. Other young women in the village, admiring Kasper's efforts, began to assist her. Soon a small but dedicated group of women were tending to the sick of Dernbach.

Katherine Kasper had no intentions of beginning a religious community, but it was through her vision and commitment to helping out her townsfolk that the Order of the Poor Handmaids of Jesus Christ was born.

The Poor Handmaids had made such a name for themselves that when Bishop Luers of the Fort Wayne Diocese wanted someone to care for the largely German population that had settled in Northern Indiana, he immediately wrote to them. In response to his request, eight Poor Handmaids made the long and sometimes perilous journey across the Atlantic and finally arrived in Hessen Castle, Indiana, in 1868. The area was quickly growing, and soon three Poor Handmaids traveled to Mishawaka.

The Sisters established St. Agnes Convent and began serving, mostly as home healthcare workers, around 1878. Soon it became apparent that the growing city needed a proper hospital. Construction on St. Joseph Hospital began in June of 1909 and within a year the hospital opened with forty beds and five nuns serving as nurses. Sister Columba served as the hospital's first administrator. In 1916 a maternity ward was added. Before long the tiny hospital needed more beds, so another wing was added in 1918. More patients required more nurses, so Sister Columba opened the School of Nursing in 1919.

Over the years the Poor Handmaids served as nurses less and less and ended up serving mostly in administrative positions. The commitment to personal care that they began, however, has always been the heart of St. Joseph's.

One nun, however, seems to have extended her watchful care into the afterlife.

Both staff and patients have seen the spectral nun, who, on many occasions, has visited the fifth floor of the surgical wing. Often nurses went into a room to check on their patients only to have them ask about the Sister who had visited them. On at least one occasion, the nun even prayed with her thankful patient. Each time the Sister was reported seen, nurses checked only to find that no nun was present in the ward at the time. Plus, the nun in question was dressed in an old fashioned habit, one that hadn't been used in decades.

The unknown Sister has caused no fear or anxiety. It's quite the opposite, in fact. Patients reported that they felt better after being visited by the nun in the old fashioned habit. One went to far as to suggest that the Sister "took away his pain."

Kevin Geisel was a patient at St. Joseph's in April of 1993. As reported by Mark Marimen in the book *Haunted Indiana 2,* Geisel was in the hospital for abdominal surgery. He recovered quickly and became bored, not used to having so much rest time. Geisel was often out of bed, wandering around and chatting with nurses. One night as he lay in bed trying to drift off to sleep, his door opened and a nun in an outdated habit walked in to check on him. Seeing he was okay, she withdrew. Later, Geisel asked a nurse about the Sister who had checked up on him. She told Geisel that he must have been mistaken, for no nuns were present on the surgical floor. When he persisted, she told him that the hospital's ghost must have paid him a visit.

Marimen also reports that the ghost comforted relatives of patients as well. One woman stayed at the hospital in her husband's room. The doctor's weren't sure that her husband would survive the night. The woman sat in a chair at her husband's bedside all night, bringing him what comfort she could. Suddenly she became aware that someone else was in the room. Looking around, she saw a nun sitting in the corner. The Sister told her that her husband would live and that everything would be all right.

Sure enough, the man recovered and lived for many more years.

The staff of St. Joseph's were generally much too busy caring for the ill to concern themselves with spectral entities. The ghostly nun did become a convenient scapegoat whenever items turned up missing. If something couldn't be located, nurses would joke that "Sister" must have taken it.

In recent years, the fifth floor has been renovated and turned into offices. With no patients to watch over, the ghostly nun seems to have vanished for good. No longer needed to keep an eye on the sick, the Sister seems to have finally retired. There are still those in the area, though, who remember the comfort they felt when Sister would enter their room to check up on them. They recall the ghostly nun with fondness, thankful that she stayed around to continue the work started all those years ago by the Poor Handmaids of Jesus Christ.

Chapter Eight
The House on Somerset

Brittany was very young when her family moved into the house on Somerset, but she'll never forget the five years they spent in that Mishawaka home. The house was on a double lot and may have been a barn at one time. The house on the front part of the lot was much larger, but the smaller three-bedroom dwelling seemed ideal for Brittany and her family. There were two bedrooms upstairs—perfect for Brittany and her older sister—and one downstairs for Mom and Dad. They quickly settled in and for a short while everything seemed fine. Soon, however, the family realized that they were *sharing* their home with some very *ACTIVE* spirits.

Brittany's mother, Elizabeth, first suspected that something odd was happening when the family went out for dinner one evening. Brittany had been playing with her collection of troll dolls and, being a typical little girl, didn't want her sister messing around with her prized possessions. Brittany insisted that her sister leave the room first so that she could line up the troll dolls so that they'd be waiting for her to play with when the family returned from their night out. When the family returned, they found that Brittany's dolls were placed in a circle with all of their heads facing inwards, the largest of the dolls placed in the center. Her daughters insisted that either Mom or Dad must have done it, while Elizabeth knew that neither she nor her husband were responsible. It was an odd moment, but not too troubling...

Then...Elizabeth began to hear a dog barking. The sound seemed to be coming from upstairs and was definitely *inside* the house. The family owned no dog, though. Following the sound, Elizabeth determined that the sound was coming from inside the closet in Brittany's room. There was also the rocking chair in Brittany's room that seemed to like to rock on its own. Elizabeth would enter the room to find the chair in motion, even on days when she knew no one had been in the room for hours.

Then...came the nightly footsteps. At the same time every night, Elizabeth could hear someone walking in the rooms above. "You could set your clock by it," she told me when I interviewed her. Upon investigation, Elizabeth could find no explanation for the noises. Everyone was accounted for, but still the footsteps could be heard...*every night at the exact same time*. Sometimes Elizabeth could hear music playing. "It was very faint and hard to make out, but you could hear it. It seemed to be coming from the walls!"

Elizabeth's husband, Scott, was a practical man. He didn't believe in ghosts and felt that there had to be some logical explanation for the sounds. After all, there was NO such thing as a haunted house. Creaky floorboards, banging pipes...there *had* to be a reasonable answer. He scoffed when Elizabeth would come to him with tales of her experiences, so she soon learned to keep quiet around Scott whenever something odd had occurred.

One day Brittany and her sister were playing when they decided to do some exploring. The closet in Brittany's bedroom was particularly large and had a wooden panel nailed in place at the back. Being curious girls, they pried the panel loose to find a small room beyond. The room seemed to be just a storage space, filled with toys, clothing, and stuffed animals, but the two girls were immediately filled with dread. Something about the room frightened them. They quickly put the wooden panel back into place.

When Elizabeth learned of the girls' anxiety over this room, she wasn't surprised. It had been from this closet, after all that Elizabeth had heard the dog barking.

The odd sounds in the house continued. If anything, they seemed to increase. Cold spots could be felt at times. Brittany and her sister could hear knocking on the floor above their heads while they were trying to sleep at night. Upstairs in the house were three small doors leading to attic-like storage spaces. The girls would wake up to find these open even though they'd been firmly closed when they'd gone to bed.

And then...the little girl began to make *her* presence known...

Elizabeth's first encounter with the ghost was on a summer day. The girls had gone to the park to play, and Elizabeth used the quiet time to clean the kitchen. She was engrossed in her work and barely noticed when she heard the front door opening. Elizabeth heard the girls laughing as they tramped up the stairs. As she continued scrubbing, she glanced up to see a little girl through the lower pane of the kitchen window. It was a fleeting glance, so she assumed the blonde child was Brittany. Shortly after this, her other daughter and a friend bounded into the kitchen seeking refreshments. Elizabeth asked about Brittany.

"She's still down at the park," her daughter replied.

Elizabeth froze. She knew she'd seen a little girl in the window. If it hadn't been Brittany...

That was the first of many sightings of the spirit, as Elizabeth began to feel a presence sitting next to her on the bed—some nights she could actually feel *someone* climbing into bed next to her.

Brittany remembers vividly the first time she saw the little girl. Her dad was in the bedroom sleeping while the girls and their mother sat in the living room watching television. She was laughing and enjoying the program when a creak on the stairs made her look away from the set. There, coming down the stairs, was a little girl. She had dirty blonde hair and wore an old-fashioned red dress. The girl stopped at the bottom of the stairs and paused to glance over at Brittany before quietly walking on into the bedroom where Dad was sleeping. Brittany remembers how shocked she and her sister were, but her mother merely shrugged and said, "I hope she leaves room for me in the bed."

"That moment will always stick in my mind," Brittany says today.

After that night, Brittany began to receive nocturnal visits from the ghost herself. "There were many nights when I would feel someone sitting on the side of the bed. I would open my eyes, thinking it was one of the two cats we had. Nothing would be there except a dent in the bed as if someone was sitting there." Some nights she would awaken in the middle of the night to find the little girl standing at the foot of her bed. After this went on for a few months, Brittany refused to sleep in her room and chose to sleep down in the living room. "My older sister was much braver. She stayed up in her room for most of the years we lived there."

Her sister did have her share of experiences, though. "She had a clock radio that would turn on even when unplugged and with no batteries in it," Brittany reports. The clock radio would often be found in the morning on the staircase. The cord would be wrapped around the clock and it would inevitably be found on the third step. Brittany's sister also had a doll that had been bought at a garage sale, which began to frighten the two girls. Not only would the doll be found in a different spot from where they'd left it, but on some occasions the girls would see the head of the doll slowly turn on its own. Finally they put the doll in the basement, which seemed to work. The doll ceased to trouble them after that.

The small bathroom the girls used downstairs had full-length mirrors that they used to check their hair and general appearance for the beginning of their day. Often they would see dark figures in the mirror, seemingly right behind them. They'd turn, only to find nothing there.

Brittany's sister often took one of their cats, Rajah, into the bathroom with her while she bathed.

One night Brittany and her father were in the living room, watching television and playing with the cat. Finally Brittany's dad told her to let Rajah out, as the cat kept going to the door. She did so, and turned back just as her sister emerged from the bathroom with Rajah bundled in her arms! They family owned two cats, but they were of very different colors and Brittany knew that she hadn't been confused. It had been Rajah that had been at the door, crying to be let out...

The third step on the staircase also seemed to be constantly in need of repair. No matter how many times Brittany's father fixed it, several days later the wood would crack and break.

One day Elizabeth and her daughters went to visit her mother, who lived just a block away. During the visit Brittany became bored and decided to walk back to their house. Getting there, she found that her father hadn't returned home from work yet and the house was still locked tight so she waited for him on the front step. Looking around, she saw a shadow being cast on the grass by something moving around in the kitchen. She looked into the kitchen window, but could see no one there. Thinking that her father was home after all, she knocked on the door and called out to him. She could hear no one moving inside, so she checked the driveway. Her father's truck wasn't there. The house was empty.

Brittany wisely decided to go back to her grandmother's, where she informed her mother that once again the spirits were walking around their home. By the time she, her sister, and her mother returned to the house Scott had arrived home. He'd found the house locked up tight and had seen no sign that anyone had been moving through the kitchen or anywhere else for that matter. Not believing in ghosts, he put the experience down to his daughter's overactive imagination.

The amount of paranormal activity in the house was beginning to take its toll on Elizabeth. She would often feel as if someone was watching her and once, while doing the dishes, the feeling was so intense that she whirled about and shouted at the empty room, "This is my house! Leave me alone!" The sensation of being watched faded—*for the time being*.

Very often when pulling away from the house in her car, Elizabeth would see a face looking down at her from one of the upstairs windows. This happened so often that Elizabeth got into the habit of making sure she kept her eyes away from the house while leaving. Seeing the face in the window was unsettling, to say the least.

Elizabeth needed answers, so she contacted a psychic. It took some convincing to get her husband to agree, but finally he relented. On the night the psychic came, Elizabeth had her daughters stay with her mother. The psychic toured the house and told Elizabeth that she simply had too many spirits in her house. He provided Elizabeth with little information, so she arranged for another psychic investigator to visit. This time the woman who came told Elizabeth that there definitely was the ghost of a little girl haunting the house. She suggested that the family place some toys in an area where the ghost had often been seen and put talcum powder on the floor to see if they could get any footprints. They tried this but had no results.

The events taking place in the Mishawaka home were having another effect as well. Elizabeth and her husband found themselves drifting apart. Today, Elizabeth isn't sure if the turmoil in the family brought about an increase in the paranormal activity or if the ghostly happenings were causing the strain in their marriage. In either case, Elizabeth eventually asked for a divorce. Soon she and her daughters packed up and moved into her mother's house, leaving Scott in the house on Somerset. This kept the girls close by so they could visit their father often.

An uncle, Tom, also living at the time with Elizabeth's mother, had been given a key to the house on Somerset by Scott just in case he ever got tired of the kids and needed some time away. The uncle had heard of the supernatural happenings experienced by the girls, but didn't believe in ghosts. One night he decided to take Scott up on his offer. Tom let himself in, and, since Scott was away, reclined on the couch intending to enjoy a peaceful evening watching television. Before long, however, he began to hear footsteps upstairs. Puzzled, Tom checked upstairs, thinking that he'd been mistaken that he was alone in the house. There was no one up there. He had barely settled back onto the couch when a hall door slammed shut.

Now thoroughly unnerved, he quickly left the house, later telling Scott that he appreciated the offer, but wouldn't be staying there ever again!

Scott eventually had his own experience. He was watching television one night when he looked up to see a young blonde girl staring at him through the front porch window. Scott's face drained of color as she *vanished* right in front of him. The next time he saw Elizabeth he simply said, "I believe you now." Later Scott rearranged the furniture so that he could watch television out of sight of the front porch window, just in case the little girl decided to make another appearance.

Elizabeth finally asked the woman who lived in the house on the front part of the lot if anything unusual happened in her place. The woman reported that she, too, had many similar experiences. Once she'd been pulled down the stairs by her ankles by some invisible force. She said that after that she'd called the elders of her church in to bless her home. She didn't reveal if this had stopped the experiences or not. Talking with other neighbors, Elizabeth learned that many years ago a murder had occurred on the property. According to their stories, a man who'd lived in the front house killed his entire family. One daughter, a little girl with dirty blonde hair, ran in terror to the back house to hide. The father caught up with her and killed her on the staircase...

...on the third step, the one that refused to stay repaired.

Chapter Nine

A Ghost Tour of Northern Indiana

Some ghosts don't seem to have a history, or if they do no one is privy to the information. There are many tales of haunts that have little or no back story. The ghost of a woman in a black shawl who seems to be searching for a lost child haunts a local road—no one knows the woman's name or why she haunts that particular locale. She's just there, and people check out the area in hopes of catching sight of her.

With this and other spirits in mind, let's take a quick ghost tour of South Bend and northern Indiana. Many of these ghosts can be found listed on TheShadowlands.net. The Shadowlands is an excellent site to check out, providing state-by-state listings of ghosts and haunted locations, along with personal accounts of paranormal activity.

Council Oak Cemetery

Our tour starts off in South Bend's Council Oak Cemetery, also known as Highland Cemetery. An eerie place by day, Council Oak Cemetery takes on a new life entirely at night. Nocturnal visitors are said to often hear the hoof beats of a phantom horse.

There's an old trail that leads to a bridge, which takes you across Juday Creek. At night, people often catch sight of what appears to be a ghostly train engineer. The spirit roams the area, holding his lantern. According to legend, the engineer committed suicide and now is doomed to haunt the bridge.

State Theater Lounge

The State Theater Lounge is said to be haunted by a woman in a white or lavender dress. She appears to be either a flapper from the 1920s or a vaudeville performer. She seems especially drawn to blues music, and can often be seen when a blues act is performing at the Lounge!

Holiday Inn

The Holiday Inn at City Center is said to be haunted by the ghost of a flight attendant. Airline staff who've stayed at the hotel have reported seeing the ghost sitting on the bed looking in the mirror at them. One story says that, years ago, a pilot killed the flight attendant in one of the rooms.

North Michigan Avenue

Up on North Michigan Avenue, you may find the ghost of a woman and her dog. The woman apparently was used to walking her dog in that area and often went dangerously close to the train tracks. One night an oncoming train struck her and the dog. Today, even though the train tracks are no longer there, people have seen the ghostly woman walking her dog. On other nights you just hear her voice, calling out her dog's name.

Posey Chapel

If we head to nearby La Porte, Indiana, we find several stories connected with Posey Chapel. At times a woman can be heard singing and a spectral tune can be heard being strummed on a guitar. People have reported seeing the ghost of a nun crossing the street. Many years ago, a church supposedly was burned to the ground in the vicinity of Posey Chapel. A tree by the gated entrance is where the church's preacher hung himself, and at times passersby will see him there still, swaying in the wind. Some people have reported feeling fine while outside the fence, but on entering the property they suddenly feel anxious. While looking up the hill to the old cemetery, some have seen a strange white form, too large to be any of the gravestones.

The Hacienda Restaurant

The Hacienda Restaurant in Mishawaka has long had a reputation for being haunted. A young woman's suicide there many years ago is said to be the cause of the ghostly happenings. Rumors persist that in certain parts of the building lights go on and off mysteriously. The taps in the restrooms will turn themselves on and off. People have also reported feeling like they were being watched, especially in the women's restroom. Does the young woman still roam the Hacienda Restaurant?

Reeder Road

If we travel a bit, we find a barren stretch of road between Merrillville and Griffith Streets called Reeder Road. This desolate bit of roadway boasts the presence of a vanishing hitchhiker. The tale is a familiar one, but if you find yourself driving down Reeder on a dark, rainy night in the vicinity of the old Ross Cemetery you might want to keep your eyes peeled for a young woman in an out-of-date dress. She may ask you for a ride. If you give her one, she will vanish before you reach the destination she gave you. As you pass Ross Cemetery, she'll *disappear* from your car...going back, apparently, to the home she's known for many years—Ross Cemetery. Other apparitions have been seen along Reeder Road, which is reputed to have been a dumping ground for dead bodies! Gangsters of the 1930s are said to have used the remote area to dispose of unwanted corpses. Animal parts are also said to be found in the center of the road. It's never the whole animal, like road kill, just a leg or perhaps the head of the animal. Once the head of a dog was sitting as if placed in the road. There was no blood, just the head of the dog sitting as if it was looking down the center of Reeder Road...

U.S. 421 at 50 North

If we travel to nearby Michigan City and get off U.S. 421 at 50 North, we'll pass an abandoned white house. Listen carefully. Are those moans and screams we can hear? According to local legend, the man who lived there killed his entire family and buried them in the basement. At times you can still hear their death cries. Be forewarned, however—sometimes the house is there, but sometimes it vanishes into thin air...

Old Lighthouse Museum

Also in Michigan City we'll find Indiana's Old Lighthouse Museum which is haunted, some believe, by the ghost of Harriet Colfax. Colfax was the lighthouse keeper from 1861 to 1904. It was her job to make the forty-foot climb up the tower every day to maintain the light. According to some, she still makes the journey up the steps to polish the reflectors and trim the wick.

Valparaiso University

Valparaiso, Indiana, is home to several ghostly legends. One tale concerns Alumni Hall at Valparaiso University, where the spirits of two young children are said to run up and down the corridors around 2 o'clock in the morning. If one manages to catch the ghosts in a talkative mood, they'll simply tell you that they're playing tag.

In his book *Ghost Stories of Indiana,* author Edrick Thay tells of a haunted house in Valparaiso where, long ago, the father of the house decided to kill his entire family. On waking the next morning neighbors were shocked to see several human heads impaled on fence posts. Upon investigation, several other heads were found placed on the mantel over the fireplace. The father had decapitated his wife and children and then shot and killed himself. Since that fateful day, visitors brave enough to trespass on the property have reported seeing severed heads appear both on the mantel and on the grounds where the fence one stood. The heads quickly vanish, but not before scaring the unwary half to death. The blood and the wounds look fresh, as if the father had just carried out his evil deed.

Peaceful Acres

In Bunker Hill, home to Grissom Air Force Base, there is a mobile home court called Peaceful Acres. A ghost wearing a bandanna and known to the locals as "the toothless wonder" haunts the nearby woods. He's sometimes seen near Lot 3, hovering over a chicken coop, looking down hungrily.

Selysions Private School

Selysions Private School in Cedar Lake had quite a legend surrounding it. According to the story, the minister who ran the all-boys school went crazy one day and murdered all of his charges, either hanging, shooting, or drowning them. For years people said that if you dared to go near the abandoned building orbs would fly right at you. The terrified screams of the boys could sometimes be heard. Looking in one of the windows, one might even catch sight of the boys at their desks, writing out their lessons in blood. The building has since been demolished, hopefully putting an end to the haunting.

Hebron's Ghosts

The high school in Hebron, Indiana, is said to be haunted by the ghost of a young girl who committed suicide in the restroom by hanging herself. Some teachers have reported hearing voices coming from that restroom when they've had to stay late.

Hebron also is reputed to have a haunted railroad track. It seems that long ago there was a train wreck and those who died still wander the site of their deaths.

Sawmill Lake

Sawmill Lake at Leesburg has a haunted house. There's a white house around the point of the lake where strange apparitions and odd vapors have been witnessed. The locals have nicknamed the ghost "Whitey." He's often heard bellowing and cursing into the night. "Whitey" may not have actually ever lived here. According to one story, he was driving drunk one night and crashed into the house. His spirit is now forever doomed to haunt the place.

Hayloft Restaurant

Up until recently one could enjoy good food and friendly service at the Hayloft Restaurant in Plymouth. The owners had taken an old barn and converted it into an eatery known for its prime rib, barbecued baby back ribs, and *Homer, the ghost*. Homer, as the staff dubbed their spirit, was often seen in the kitchen and dining room and even occasionally outside the restaurant. Homer seemed to float everywhere, since whenever he manifested everything was visible except his feet. Patrons and staff always knew when Homer was ready to make a visit, because the smell of wet, burned wood always preceded him. Perhaps Homer was trying to warn the owners of what was to come. The Hayloft Restaurant was heavily damaged by fire in April 2001 and had to close its doors.

Leo's Ghosts

Leo, Indiana, has a few ghosts as well. Off Coldwater Road is a place called Cedar Canyon and the spirit of a man who appears to be in his late sixties haunts this area. Nearly transparent, the man is most often seen in the vicinity of the nearby cemetery, usually between midnight and 3 o'clock.

"The Haunted Places of Indiana" website tells of a ghost that seemed to be attached to a teacher at Leo High School. The drama teacher had transferred from another school where a girl hung herself in the auditorium. The spirit must have blamed the teacher for her suicide, for she transferred with the teacher, causing havoc during his productions. The teacher has since left Leo, presumably taking the ghost with him.

Lowell's Ghosts

In Lowell, Indiana, the legend persists that three people were brutally murdered at a nearby mansion and their bodies dumped by a bridge on Clay Street. If you stop your car on this bridge, you may find it rocked violently back and forth by unseen forces. A dense fog is also said to appear and completely surround your vehicle.

Lowell seems to be the place to drive around if you want to witness the paranormal. Another story says that if you travel east on 173rd Avenue towards Holtz Road something odd may happen. Before hitting Holtz, there will be two large hills. Upon reaching the top of the first hill, one is told to look down at the intersection of 173rd and Holtz. You may see what appears to be a terrible accident, complete with flashing lights and rescue vehicles. Coming down the hill, the sight of the accident will be blocked by the second hill. Once you crest the second hill, however, all signs of the accident will have vanished. No lights. No smashed cars. Nothing.

Grand Kankakee Marsh County Park

Another tale concerns Grand Kankakee Marsh County Park. Located along the Kankakee River, the densely wooded area was once, according to the story, the site of a large mansion. An old woman, whose name is unknown, built the house, but had no idea that she was building on sacred Indian burial grounds. She soon learned of her folly, however, when she began to see Indian figures surrounded by mist in the woods around her property. A lone female Indian was spotted most often, sometimes just walking around the woods, but more often sitting by a tree as if waiting for someone. These sights so disturbed the old woman that she sold her mansion and property to the park. The mansion is long gone, but visitors may still catch sight of the Indian woman. It's said that couples are especially likely to see her. When driving into the park, the ghostly woman has been known to gaze wistfully into car windows at young couples, leading some to believe that she's looking for her own lost love.

Renssalaer's Ghosts

We end our tour in Renssalaer, where we find two cemeteries across from each other on the road leading out of town. Years ago, in true Romeo and Juliet style, a pair of young lovers were forbidden to see each other. The families involved had been feuding for years. Dejected, the young couple committed suicide. Their suicide notes pleaded that they be buried side by side, but neither family could agree to this so they were buried across the road from each other. Legend tells us that if you stop your car between the cemeteries you'll see a young brunette woman in white and a young man in black cross the road to meet each other. Be warned, though. The young woman was brought up in a strict, religious family. If she hears you cuss, the spirits will attack your car!

†††††††††††††††

A La Porte Haunting

Located just a short drive from South Bend is the city of La Porte. First settled in 1830, La Porte had previously been a favorite camping ground for the Potawatomi Indians. As Beth Scott and Michael Norman recount in their book *Haunted Heartland,* the Potawatomi were particularly drawn to the pond near what is now I and 10th Streets which they dubbed "Came and Went." After a heavy rain, the pond would be full, but at other times it would dry to almost nothing, thus "Came and Went." As the settlers pushed the Native Americans further and further west, the Potawatomis often stopped by Came and Went on their way to Kansas. It was here that a young Potawatomi girl grew sick and died.

According to some, her spirit is responsible for the haunting of not just one but two buildings.

When Dr. George Andrew completed his medical studies in Ohio and New York, he came to La Porte to open up his medical practice. He married Catherine Piatt Andrew, a distant cousin and the daughter of one of La Porte's founders. The doctor began construction in 1845 on a home for his bride, a large Colonial mansion that would be one of the finest structures in the midwest.

Dr. Andrew was one of the first physicians to use ether in surgery. During the Civil War, he served in the Army of the Potomac and the Army of the West. He returned to his mansion at the end of the war and retired from his medical practice in 1885. Dr. Andrew died in 1911. His wife died in 1926, having reached the age of one hundred.

The Dunn family purchased the house from the Andrews in 1885 and lived there until 1904. It was then that the Gwynne family settled into the home. Soon after moving into the house, the Gwynnes began to wonder if they were the only inhabitants.

Madeline Gwynne Kinney was a daughter in the household and would later become curator of the La Porte County Historical Museum. She was the first to notice paranormal activity in the house.

Kinney was busy one day cleaning an empty downstairs closet. Satisfied with her work, she gathered up her cleaning supplies and was ready to exit when she heard a strange tinkling sound behind her. Turning around, she was surprised to find several coins on the floor of the closet. The coins were from the 1860s and 1870s. She searched the closet, but could find no cracks in the walls or ceiling. The coins seemed to have fallen out of the air.

Her father was the next person to have an unusual experience. One snowy night, Mr. Gwynne had settled by the fire to enjoy a book when suddenly the front doorbell jangled. Gwynne frowned, wondering who could be calling at such a late hour and in such inclement weather. The bell continued to ring, so Gwynne rose and went to the door, but on opening it he discovered that no one was there. Not only that, but the snow leading up to the house was undisturbed. Gwynne checked the bell, which was one that had to be twisted to produce a ring. Everything seemed to be in order. Gwynne concluded that his visitor was not of this world...

The Gwynne family continued to live in the mansion until 1948 and grew used to hearing ghostly footsteps sounding up and down the stairs. Windows were often found open in the mornings after being firmly secured the night before. The Gwynnes didn't seem to mind sharing their home with unseen specters. As Madeline Gwynne Kinney was later to observe, it made life interesting. They never knew what the spirits would be up to next!

The house eventually was purchased by the Zimmerman family, who lived there from 1958 to 1963. The Zimmermans also experienced supernatural happenings, but were less enthused about the occurrences than the Gwynnes had been. The father of the house was so disturbed by the nightly footsteps that he purchased a gun for protection!

One of the daughters of the house had a similar experience to that of Madeline Gwynne Kinney. Cleaning the same closet, she also found old coins seemingly appearing from nowhere. Again, the coins were nearly a hundred years old...

Another daughter, Ginna, was out one fine spring day picking flowers in the garden. Suddenly a chill came over her and she had the distinct impression that she was being watched. She looked up at the house to see the figure of a woman in one of the attic windows. Ginna went back in the house and checked out the room, only to find an obviously unused room. No one had been in the room for years, as shown by the coating of dust and grime on the floor. No footprints showed in the dust, and, checking with the family, Ginna learned that no visitors had come to the house that day.

The Potawatomi girl may not be the only spirit that haunted the old Andrew Mansion. A tale is told of two women who lived in the house in the late nineteenth century. One of the women fell in love with a man who left her to make his fortune out in California, where the Gold Rush was making men rich overnight. He vowed that if she waited for him, he'd return to La Porte and share his wealth with her. Whether or not he followed through on his promise isn't reported, but it hardly mattered. A few days after his departure, the woman was killed when a train hit a carriage she was riding in. Her spirit remained at the house, waiting in vain for her love to return to her.

The Andrew Mansion was torn down in the early 1970s and a medical center was built on the site. The ghosts that roamed the house seem to have switched dwellings, as the paranormal occurrences continue at the medical center. The elevator especially seems to have a mind of its own, moving between floors and opening and closing even though no one has pushed any call buttons. Custodians have come to work in the morning to find the restrooms locked from the inside—restrooms that don't have windows or another exit.

Whatever had haunted the Andrew home seems to be attached to the land, not to the dwelling itself. The ghostly activity continues to this day, and shows no sign of slowing down. For years to come people visiting I and 10th Streets may feel that there is someone standing just behind them... *someone NOT of this world.*

Chapter Ten
The Tale of the Black Widow

Looking at her description or photographs, it is difficult to imagine Belle Gunness in the role of a seductress. A big woman weighing in the neighborhood of 280 pounds, Gunness sports a stern look in photos. In her role as one of the nation's most notorious female mass murderers, Gunness is also unusual. Poison was usually the weapon of choice for her contemporaries such as Jane Tappan, Lydia Sherman, and Sarah Jane Robinson, but Belle wasn't averse to using strychnine to kill. Her first husband and several of her children most likely met their fates by strychnine poisoning, but the majority of her victims were butchered with an axe.

Born Bella Poulsdatter in 1859 in Trondhjeim, Norway, details of her early life are sketchy. One unconfirmed story states that in her late teens Belle became pregnant. The father of her child, a young man of higher birth – Belle, after all, was just a farmer's daughter – became enraged when she came to tell him of the pregnancy. He beat the young woman badly, causing her to abort the child. Several days later the young man vanished and was never seen again. If this story is true, he was the first victim of Belle Gunness.

In 1883 Belle sailed to America, using money sent to her by an older sister who had earlier emigrated and was now married and living in Chicago. Belle stayed with her sister for a while. It was in Chicago that Belle met Mads Sorenson. The two soon married. Over the next sixteen years the couple adopted three children, Jennie, Myrtle, and Lucy.

The Sorensons opened a candy shop in Chicago, but business was poor. Strangely, just weeks before the Sorensons would have had to close for good, their shop was destroyed by fire. Luckily it was heavily insured.

Belle may have acquired a taste for easy insurance money. In early 1900 Mads died suddenly and mysteriously. Although his symptoms closely resembled arsenic poisoning, the doctors determined that the relatively young Norwegian had died of a heart attack. This occurred just when two insurance policies overlapped, and Belle received nearly $8,000 to help her get over her grief, a large sum for those days.

Belle used her money to buy a farm in La Porte. The place had formerly been a house of prostitution run by one Mattie Altie. Altie had died of old age and the house remained vacant until Belle purchased it. The neighbors were pleased. Belle, who seemed friendly and hard-working, would erase the stigma that Altie had brought to the area.

Workers who assisted Belle in restoring the property did find a few of her demands puzzling. Why did Belle need a six-foot fence topped with barbed wire around her hog pen? Just what was so special about this small area, and why was she so insistent that the pen be just right?

It mattered little, for the town was pleased Belle was there. They were even happier when, seemingly out of the blue, she produced a new husband, farmer Peter Gunness. Gunness, a widower, also brought into the family his young son from his previous marriage.

Within months, Peter Gunness' son became ill and died.

The boy's father himself died at the end of 1900 when, according to the story Belle told the authorities, a large cast iron meat grinder fell off a shelf and struck Gunness right between the eyes. Months later an inquest was held, during which Belle wept convincingly. Although the sheriff and coroner were suspicious, unable to come up with any reasonable explanation for the meat grinder falling off the shelf, a verdict of accidental death was issued.

The Tale of the Black Widow

Perhaps people should have paid more attention to little Myrtle Gunness when she told a school friend that her mother had killed her father. According to Myrtle, Belle "hit him with a cleaver and he died."

After the death of Peter Gunness, the farm began to prosper, although Belle seemed to have trouble keeping farmhands. Some would stay for a few months, but would then vanish overnight—never to be seen or heard from again.

Then Belle hired on Ray Lamphere. A good worker but maybe a little slow in the mind, Lamphere soon seemed to become more than just a hired hand to Belle. The hefty woman was often seen in town arm-in-arm with the small, thin Lamphere.

The romance apparently died out quickly, however, as Belle was then seen in the company of other men. Gunness had begun to put personal advertisements in newspapers around the Midwest, looking for a suitable husband to help her run the farm. These suitors would arrive at the Gunness homestead, but none of them seemed to stick around long.

One such suitor, Andrew Helgelein, was even spotted at a La Porte bank, arranging to have his life savings withdrawn from his bank in South Dakota. He and Belle, he announced happily to anyone who would listen, were getting married.

Less than a week after this, Helgelein, like those before him, disappeared overnight. A tearful Belle confided to neighbors that she had no luck with men.

A Missouri man, George Anderson, answered Belle's ad. He arrived at the farm with $300 cash in his pockets. Belle seemed to like him, but was concerned about money. Anderson started to become suspicious when Belle implored him to return to Missouri and sell his farm. Once he had all of his money, Belle told him, he could return and they could begin their lives together. Anderson became even more suspicious that night when he awoke to find the big woman standing next to his bed, a cold, heartless look on her face. The frightened Anderson took the first train back to his farm in Tarkio, swearing he'd never set foot on the Gunness farm again.

During this time Lamphere was often found at the local bars, drinking and swearing that one day he would get even with the woman who had tossed him aside.

Belle hired Joe Maxon, a La Porte man, as a new hand. Maxon was given the room above the kitchen, where he generally kept to himself when he wasn't toiling on the farm. Maxon often spotted Lamphere at a distance, lurking just down the road or behind some trees. Belle's ex-farmhand seemed unable to keep away from the property.

On April 27, 1908 Belle went to a lawyer to draw up her last will and testament. She told the lawyer that Lamphere was out to get her and that she feared the man would burn her house to the ground.

Early the following morning, the house was indeed destroyed by fire. The bodies of the Gunness children were found as well as that—presumably—of Belle. It was hard to tell if the body was actually Belle. The body was headless.

In the days after the blaze, odd things began to be found in the rubble. Several men's watches and wallets, emptied, were uncovered. Then a human rib cage was unearthed. An arm bone was discovered, and then an entire human skeleton.

Belle's suitors had finally been located.

Asle Hegelein, brother of the missing Andrew, came to town to assist in the digging, fearing the worst. Working with Maxon and another man, Asle unearthed a gunnysack near the hog pen. Inside were his brother's remains. Andrew Hegelein had been hacked to pieces. The men continued to dig, uncovering four more bodies that day, all in the pigpen area.

One of the bodies found was that of Jennie, Belle's adopted daughter, who had supposedly gone off to college in California. Eventually over forty bodies of men and children were found.

Despite growing belief that Belle had murdered the dozens of bodies that were found on the farm, Ray Lamphere was charged with murder. On May 12th, Belle's dentures were located. The coroner pronounced Gunness dead, even though her head had yet to be found and one of the leading doctors in town was still insisting that the headless body was much too small to be Belle's.

Ray Lamphere was indicted for the murders of the Gunness family on May 22. During the trial that followed, evidence was brought forward revealing that days before the fire Belle had been seen in the company of a strange woman. While not quite as large as Belle, the woman was indeed stout. No one knew who the woman was, other than the fact that she came from Chicago, or what had become of her.

A defense witness also claimed to have seen Gunness *after* the fire. Although admitting that he'd only seen the woman at a distance, the witness insisted that he recognized Belle, who was in the company of a man. The witness tried to follow the couple, but they hurried away and the witness was unable to catch up. A toxicology professor, Dr. Walter Haines, also testified that he had found lethal amounts of strychnine in the bodies of the Gunness children.

The jury found Lamphere guilty of arson, but not of murder. They believed Lamphere was responsible for the fire, but that Belle had already killed her children and then committed suicide. No explanation for the body being headless was given. Lamphere was sentenced to two to twenty-one years and sent to the state penitentiary in Michigan City. There he often told his cellmate that Belle had fooled them all. The murderess was still out there, Lamphere claimed. She had beheaded the woman from Chicago and left the body to be identified as herself. Lamphere himself was to meet back up with Belle a few days after the fire, but the woman had tricked him as well. Lamphere did not languish long in prison. The little man contracted tuberculosis and died December 30, 1909.

The townsfolk now believed that Lamphere had assisted Gunness in the murders. The big mystery, though, was whether Lamphere burned down the farm or if Belle had set the blaze herself. The populace was divided, with some believing that Belle had died in the fire (with Lamphere, for some reason, taking away her head) and others thinking that Belle was indeed still alive.

Some believe that Belle was heard from again. A woman in Los Angeles was arrested for murder in 1931. The woman, known as Esther Carlson, was accused of poisoning August Lindstrom for money. She died awaiting trial. The description certainly fit that of Gunness, but with the Great Depression straining funds, the authorities in La Porte couldn't afford to check into the matter further.

Recently the body supposed to be that of Belle Gunness was exhumed so that DNA tests could, once and for all, show whether Belle died in the fire or faked her own death. At the time of this writing, the results are still unknown. However, solving the mystery of the headless body won't put an end to the Belle Gunness story. The tales will live on...

Belle Gunness & the Paranormal

One Investigator's Experiences

Marcus Griffin stood alone in Patton Cemetery near the grave of Andrew Helgelein, one of the last victims of Belle Gunness. Suddenly, he could hear faint voices. He'd just looked up in the sky and said to himself, "Oh, look. The Big Dipper." A voice answered back, "Shhh! The Big Dipper!"

There was no one standing anywhere around him.

Griffin had his first paranormal experience when he was six or seven years old. It was the middle of summer, and his mother had locked the house up so that she could stock up at the grocery store. He remembers that he was standing in his sister's bedroom and very clearly heard a woman's voice yelling his name from the bottom of the stairs. He got cold chills hearing the voice, knowing that no one could have entered the house. Because of that moment, every detail of his sister's room is imprinted on his memory.

He later learned from his father that paranormal activity had been going on in the home for quite some time. The house was new, having been built by his grandfather and father when Griffin was a toddler. He theorizes that the haunting was connected to the land the house was built on, or that he himself could have been a catalyst for poltergeist activity.

The sump pump cover in the laundry room would be in place one minute, only to be found across the room moments later. Griffin's father also heard a disembodied female voice in the house saying, "Just one more game, Bill. Just one more game."

Griffin's interest in the paranormal continued. In his early twenties he began to occasionally spot what he refers to as a Shadow Spirit. The figure appeared to him in a gray form, but others, including his wife Becca, have seen it more clearly. According to her and others, the gray man looks just like Griffin himself, only much older. "It's him, but more like seventy years of age," she reports.

Several years ago Griffin formed WISP, or Witches in Search of the Paranormal. Together with Becca, who considers herself a witch, Griffin investigates with two Wiccan practitioners, Tina and Tim. Griffin feels that the metaphysical skills they've developed gives them an edge in paranormal investigations. Griffin isn't out to prove that ghosts exist—*he already knows they do*. For him, it's the interaction that interests him.

While researching on the Internet, Griffin came across the Belle Gunness story. He'd previously known of the Gunness case, but hadn't realized that the murders had taken place less than an hour's drive from his home in Elkhart. Griffin searched for any paranormal experiences connected with the Gunness murders, but could only find a mention of an EVP a woman had gathered at Patton Cemetery. He and the team did some heavy research and learned that the foundation of Belle's farm was used to build another house. Using descriptions of the area found in newspaper articles of the time, they finally tracked down the house. Unfortunately, the present owner refused to give them permission to hold an investigation there. Griffin did, however, get an odd sensation just standing on the property. "It's a feeling that you can't put into words," he says. "Of course, knowing what happened there...it just gave me an odd feeling."

The team next visited Patton Cemetery. As was their usual routine, the first trip was taken during daylight hours. Griffin feels that it's important to know the lay of the land and any possible difficulties before checking out the location at night. At first, it seemed like finding the grave of Andrew Helgelein would be an impossible task. Vandals had apparently visited the graveyard and many of the headstones had been toppled, including that of Helgelein. Luckily that stone was knocked over so that the inscription was face up, otherwise the team wouldn't have found it. Griffin had read that the graves of Belle's husband Peter Gunness and her daughter Jennie Olsen were supposed to be right by that of Helgelein, but they couldn't be located. Griffin later learned that their graves were unmarked.

WISP's first night investigation of Patton Cemetery was held the following weekend. They started off at the grave of Helgelein, hoping to catch some EVPs. Griffin and his team kept their recorders going throughout the investigation, enabling them to check what each recorder is picking up at the same time. In this fashion Griffin has been able to dismiss several false EVPs by identifying the sound as coming from another member of the team.

Nothing seemed to be happening, however, until Becca noticed a dark figure darting between two headstones some ways off. The team went to investigate, leaving Griffin on his own. It was then that he began to hear whispered voices.

Along with the Big Dipper comment, other voices were caught on Griffin's recorder. A male voice could be heard saying, "Body back there." A female voice responded, saying, "I know."

His wife Becca had an unnerving experience in the cemetery as well. As she and Tim were walking along, they heard an unearthly growl. It didn't sound human or like any animal Becca knew of. The source of the growl couldn't be found.

Griffin isn't willing to say that he communicated with the ghosts of Peter Gunness, Andrew Helgelein, or Jennie Olsen at Patton Cemetery. Since the voices caught on the digital recorders don't identify themselves by name, Griffin isn't sure whom the voices belong to. He is, however, convinced that Patton Cemetery is haunted, particularly in the area around the graves of Gunness and the others.

Griffin, who has served as an expert consultant on the paranormal aspects of the Gunness case, doesn't believe the body found in the remains of the burned farmhouse is that of Belle. "It just doesn't wash," he states. He believes that Belle ended her life under the name of Esther Carlson, awaiting trial in a Los Angeles jail cell.

For Marcus Griffin, the investigation of any paranormal activity surrounding the case of Belle Gunness is far from over. He intends to return to Patton Cemetery with his team to see what else they can find and hopes to soon be able to check out the actual site of the murders. There is more to be learned about this fascinating case, he feels...and the dead can reveal so much.

††††††††††††††

Becca's Story

Becca's first brush with the paranormal was what she now laughingly refers to as "the Dinosaur Experience."

She was fourteen at the time and staying at her grandmother's house. As all the adults in the household were going out for the evening, Becca was given the task of babysitting her two younger cousins. Becca got the younger girls into bed and was preparing for a quiet evening watching television or reading while waiting for the grownups to return when a boom seemed to shake the house.

She barely had time to look around her before another boom followed. After a short pause, there was a third. The pounding continued, getting louder each time. Knick-knacks began to fall off of shelves. The sounds were so loud that Becca thought of a dinosaur walking past the house. Impossible, she knew, but she could think of no other explanation for the sounds. It wasn't the steady rumble of an earthquake, but more the sound of a giant taking an early evening constitutional.

The noise woke Becca's young charges, who came screaming out of the bedroom. Just about then the thumps began to lessen in intensity until they faded away altogether.

Becca never found an explanation for the phenomenon, but other events took place in the house. An aunt one time came screaming, naked, out of the bathroom. She had disrobed and was preparing to step into the bath when suddenly the water came slashing up as if some invisible force was getting into the bath ahead of her!

Another incident involved the numerous pipes smoked by Becca's grandfather and her Uncle Levi. One day all the pipes in the ashtrays in the house mysteriously disappeared, only to be found later in Uncle Levi's room. No one had an explanation of how they got there.

Years later, Becca had gathered up several photos of her father and put them in an album. When, days later, she opened the book and found the pictures in question missing she was quite shocked. She searched in vain, but no trace of the photographs could be found. Three months later the pictures re-appeared. She found them in the middle of her bed as she was making it one day. Recalling the incident, she laughed. "I know I didn't sleep on them for three months!"

Today Becca is very comfortable with the notion of the paranormal. Her past experiences have taught her that there is little to fear from the unseen realm. That doesn't mean, however, that ghosts and the like don't startle her now and then!

The grave of John Dillinger in Crown Hill Cemetery, Indianapolis.

Chapter Eleven
Jailhouse
& Graveyard Specters

Crown Point Jail

A jailhouse is a likely spot for a haunting. After all, what jail hasn't had a history of suffering or even death?

Certainly spirits seem to haunt the old Crown Point Jail.

Crown Point Jail is famous for the escape of bank robber John Dillinger in 1934. Prior to Dillinger's dramatic exit, the jail had been thought escape-proof. The myths and legends concerning the breakout abound. Famously, a story recounts how Dillinger carved a bar of soap into the shape of a gun and then blacked the soap using shoe polish. Another tale says that he whittled a gun out of a block of wood.

The most likely explanation is that his attorney, Louis Piquett, smuggled a real gun in to Dillinger.

The escape seemed to be well planned. Brandishing the gun, Dillinger and another inmate, an African American by the name of Herbert Youngblood, escaped through the jail's kitchen area. They got to the Main Street Garage where they disabled two cars and stole the remaining vehicle—a 1933 Ford V8 belonging to Crown Point's Sheriff Lillian Holley.

The forty-two-year old Holley, incensed over this outrage, later said that if she ever set eyes on Dillinger again she'd shoot him with her own gun.

Dillinger and Youngblood took two hostages with them; one of them was garage mechanic Edwin Saagar, whom Dillinger forced to drive the escape vehicle. The criminals made their way to Chicago, where Dillinger met up with his girlfriend, Evelyn "Billie" Frechette.

Dillinger loved hearing the stories and tall tales told of his escape. He particularly liked the wooden gun story and often repeated it himself, adding to the already growing legend.

Dillinger met his eventual end at the hands of FBI agent Melvin Purvis. Purvis and his fellow agents had been on Dillinger's track for months and finally gunned the criminal down outside the Biograph Theater in Chicago. Dillinger is buried in Crown Point Cemetery in Indianapolis.

It's unknown if the paranormal happenings at the old jail are connected with Dillinger, but many people have reported seeing lights go on and off in the building. Orbs often show up in photographs, and visitors have heard unexplained voices and the rattling of jail bars. Some have reported hearing the cell doors slamming. Strangely, a phantom dog has also been heard barking in the building.

Several locations in Crown Point, including the old jail, were used in the filming of director Michael Mann's film "Public Enemy," which stars Johnny Depp as Dillinger. The making of the film brought national attention to Crown Point once again as, for a few days, Hollywood took over the small town. There were no reports of ghostly activity during the filming. Perhaps the spirits were watching as the crew transformed the old jail back to its heyday of the 1930s and decided to keep quiet.

We may never know if John Dillinger's ghost haunts the old Crown Point Jail or if the spirit activity is due to some other soul who seems unwilling to vacate the spot. Dillinger certainly was proud of his escape...maybe so proud that he doesn't want to leave, even after death.

†††††††††††††

The Gypsies Graveyard

According to the legend, a band of gypsies came through the area that would later be Crown Point around 1820. They set up camp just southeast of the town, much to the consternation of the local farmers. The farmers didn't like the look of the swarthy gypsies. They worried that their livestock would be stolen and that the gypsies would practice witchcraft or worse. When the Romany came to town to trade, they were therefore shunned. The gypsy women weren't even allowed to buy food.

The fall of 1820 was particularly harsh and brought with it an outbreak of influenza. Several in the gypsy encampment fell deathly ill, and the lack of food and medicine didn't help. Several of the gypsy leaders again came to town, begging for medicine. They were again turned down.

In the days that followed, many of the gypsies died. The dead were buried in simple, unmarked graves. Fearful that the disease would spread into the town, several men went to the gypsy encampment to insist that the Romany leave the area. The gypsies protested, saying they were too sick and unprepared for a long journey. The townspeople were adamant, however, and gave the gypsies two days to vacate.

Days later, the farmers were pleased to see the gypsy caravan heading down the road. When they went to the encampment to make sure that all the Romany had left all they found were the mounds of earth marking where the dead were buried. Satisfied, the farmers returned to their homes, only to find that the bottoms of their pants were wet not from dew but blood—the gypsies had left a curse on the town.

Today the gypsy burial ground is more properly called South East Grove Cemetery. It's said that if you visit the graveyard at night, the bottom of your pants will be soaked red. Apparitions have been seen amongst the stones, orbs have been known to chase people out of the cemetery, and a Bible brought into the graveyard will burst into flames.

Jailhouse & Graveyard Specters: The Gypsies Graveyard

Most of the tale is almost certainly urban legend. There are no historical records showing that gypsies had visited the area in the 1820s. In fact, there wasn't even a town at that time. It wasn't until 1834 that, according to the timeline on CrownPoint.net, Solon Robinson and his family staked a claim to the land that would eventually be Crown Point. The Robinsons were the first settlers of the area, a good fourteen years after the influenza outbreak that reportedly wiped out the gypsy camp.

Still, the story persists. Visitors to the cemetery like to go to the back area where the gypsies were originally buried (although some insist the gypsy graves are actually outside the graveyard, beyond the back fence). Others are skeptical. As one local put it, "There ain't no gypsies buried out there!"

Even if the story isn't historically accurate, there does seem to be paranormal activity associated with the Gypsies Graveyard. In his book *Haunted Indiana,* Mark Marimen reports that not only were some teenagers chased out of the cemetery by a large, glowing ball of light, but that one local resident, taking a friend on a tour through the Gypsies Graveyard, had an unnerving experience. When the two men got back to their car, one man's pant leg was stained red as if with blood. The local man's trousers had been spared—but then, he had some gypsy blood in him.

Chapter Twelve

Ghostly Theatres, Cemeteries, & Bridges

Bristol Opera House

Theater people seem by their very nature to be superstitious folk. Many of their sayings have entered into common parlance, such as "break a leg" to mean good luck. Some actors panic if anyone whistles in the dressing rooms. Actor Jimmy Durante had a fit if anyone left a hat on a bed backstage. It's also considered the worst of luck for anyone in a theater to actually mention the play "Macbeth" by name. It is generally just called the Scots play!

Ghosts are also a fairly common theater phenomenon.

The Bristol Opera House, now home to the Elkhart Civic Theatre, is haunted by a ghost that they have nicknamed Percy.

Built in 1897 by Cyrus and Horace Mosier, the Bristol Opera House was meant to bring entertainment and enlightenment to the local citizens. The first production, *U.S.S. Pinafore,* was a smash success, filling the house every night. The revenues generated by the small theater, however, weren't large enough to attract the bigger, more popular acts and shows and soon Cyrus Mosier had difficulty filling all the seats. The prices of many of the traveling shows—sometimes as much as a quarter—made many of the local citizens decide to stay at home. Mosier, who also owned the local newspaper, *The Bristol Banner,* advertised his shows heavily, but the audiences continued to dwindle. Traveling medicine shows became a usual attraction at the Opera House. Around 1915, Mosier converted the building into a cinema.

In the following years, the Bristol Opera House became a music hall, a skating rink, and even a basketball court. Finally it fell into such poor repair that it was good only as a storage building. It was supposed to have been demolished in 1960, but for some reason this never happened.

A year later the Elkhart Civic Theatre leased the building. For several years ECT had been living a nomadic existence and they hoped the Bristol Opera House could be their permanent residence. The building was in horrible condition, but the thespians were determined. They bought and renovated the building and have successfully been presenting shows there for more than forty years.

Some shows have been successful despite the attempts of the mischievous ghost known as Percy. Percy, it seems, isn't fond of musicals and has been known to move things around on stage during productions. He also likes to hide in the folds of the curtain and brush up against the actors as they walk past. He particularly likes to scare women. Once one of the costumers was working late at night by herself when she felt odd things going on around her. She didn't hear anything in particular, but just *felt* that *something unseen* was in her presence. Then she felt a tap on her shoulder...

Percy seems to mainly haunt the stage and costume room, but if you're enjoying one of the fine productions given by the Elkhart Civic Theatre and you see something out of the corner of your eye...you may have just had a brush with Percy.

†††††††††††††

Little Egypt Cemetery & Troll Bridge

Just outside of Breman, Indiana, is a small graveyard listed on the maps as Ewald Cemetery. Locally it's more commonly known as Little Egypt Cemetery, and many feel that it's one of the most haunted sites in Northern Indiana.

There are many tales associated with Little Egypt: figures can be seen moving between the headstones; one tombstone glows an eerie green in the moonlight; and giggling can often be heard coming from within the locked, gated cemetery. Strands of barbed wire lines the top of the surrounding fence, so it would be difficult for anyone to get inside to play a practical joke on any nocturnal visitors. Some intrepid souls who have braved visiting the cemetery at night have reported seeing a misty figure that makes a *whooshing* sound as it goes by.

Another legend of Little Egypt, reported on TheShadowlands.net, says that when you return to your car, you'll find hand prints on the windshield. There is also the grave of a child in the cemetery—placing a nickel on the child's tombstone will result in hearing a baby cry.

Money also figures in another tale. When visiting the cemetery, you're urged to keep a penny in your left hand the entire time you're there. At the end of your vigil, you might find that you now have two pennies in your hand or even a nickel. However, if you find you've lost your penny, you'll have a restless night full of bad dreams.

On certain nights, one can hear the screams of a young girl coming from the surrounding woods, and nearby the graveyard is a tree, marking the spot where, years ago, a boy was murdered. There is a bloodstain on the tree that never fades.

A phantom farmer, who died under mysterious circumstances in the fields around Little Egypt, is said to chase visitors from the area.

Just down the road from the cemetery is a bridge known as Troll Bridge, so named because of the enormous black creature that is said to live under it. Some people have reported seeing a large black shape or shadow chasing their car as they drive across Troll Bridge. At times the smell of decaying flesh permeates the area. The remains of the troll's lunch, perhaps?

There is another story connected with this bridge. Years ago, a mentally handicapped Amish lad was taken out to the bridge by several other boys. Intending only to frighten the youngster, the boys let things get out of hand and the mentally challenged boy ended up falling off the bridge to his death. Legend tells us that your car may stall now when driving over the spot where the boy died. Some have reported not being able to re-start their vehicles until they've pushed them off the bridge entirely, where suddenly the cars start right up. If this happens, make sure you take a look back at the bridge. You may see the figure of a boy, about fourteen years of age, watching you. Don't be surprised if he vanishes before your eyes.

The ghosts of two old women driving a horse-drawn buggy are also said to haunt the area. When the South Bend Paranormal Task Force investigated Little Egypt Cemetery and Troll Bridge, they ran into a young couple that ventured out to the cemetery for thrills. The investigators asked the couple if they'd witnessed anything unusual and were told that nothing much had happened. However, on their way to Little Egypt, the couple had gotten lost and had finally pulled their car over to consult a map. While they were trying to figure out where they were, a horse-drawn buggy passed them, driven by two old women. The couple had asked the women for directions and was surprised when they received no answer. The women in the buggy acted as if they couldn't even see the young couple in their parked car.

The couple apparently was unaware of the story of the *ghost-driven buggy*.

Chapter Thirteen
Small City Haunts

Blue Cast Sanitarium

Woodburn has the distinction of being able to call itself the smallest city in Indiana. According to the 2000 census, the population of Woodburn was 1,579, consisting of 583 households. Although the building has long since been torn down, Woodburn was also once home to Blue Cast Sanitarium. This mecca of health and healing, like many such places in the 1930s and 40s, had some pretty amazing claims. According to their advertisements, a trip to the Blue Cast Sanitarium would provide relief from stomach and kidney troubles. If your system was run down, a stay at this spa would have you built back up in no time. They even promised a certain cure for rheumatism!

The pleasant surroundings and pure air were part of the cure, to be sure, but the "magnetic spring water" was what really did the trick. After almost magical treatments from the healing water and soothing mud baths, one would find all his ailments cured. Blue Cast Sanitarium claimed that no other health resort would serve a person better. They even provided free auto service to bring you to the sanitarium.

After the sanitarium closed in the 1940s the building became a natural spring water plant. This closed as well and the building remained empty until it was torn down in the 1970s. According to TheShadowlands.net, however, the story doesn't end there.

Blue Cast Sanitarium may no longer stand, but the site boasts some ghostly activity. Red glowing orbs have been spotted there, and people have seen dark shadows moving about. Shouts and other strange noises have also been heard.

Perhaps the shouts are coming from unhappy former patients at the sanitarium who found that their rheumatism wasn't cured after all.

†††††††††††††††

The Small, Haunted City of Kendallville

Kendallville is located in the northeast corner of the state, in Noble County. According to the last census, it has a population of 9,616 people over its 5.3 square miles. According to others, such as TheShadowlands.net, it also boasts a few ghostly inhabitants.

There is a church in Kendallville that has a reputation of being haunted. People have reported hearing phantom footsteps going up and down the stairs. Cold spots can often be felt. Others claim that they've seen faces behind them in mirrors, but upon turning found no one is behind them. Icy hands have touched people, and there are reports of getting scratched, or finding odd marks on their skin. Some have found mysterious bruises on their stomachs. Some have heard scratching within the walls. Marks have appeared on the walls as if by magic, and some have seen tall, dark figures moving chairs around! Tales are told of a dark shadow that can be found in the downstairs kitchen if you're alone. The shadow will slowly get closer to you until it finally chases you up the stairs where it abruptly vanishes.

Also in Kendallville is East Noble High School. East Noble educates approximately 1,200 students...and possibly holds a spirit or two. If you find yourself walking alone in the school gym, look quickly beside you—some have seen a ghostly man walking beside them. Sometimes he's been seen up in the bleachers, staring down at you.

Another legend tells of a girl who died in the science room. Janitors have turned off the television in this room only to return to find it turned back on. Turning it back off seems to do little good, because if they leave it will only be turned back on again, always set to MTV. Apparently even spirits want their MTV.

The Strand Movie Theater is said to be haunted by one of its previous owners. Over the years, there have been numerous sightings of a ghostly figure within its walls. Years ago, one of the managers had brought her kids with her while she cleaned up the place. The kids, age three and five, had fun running around the theater and soon the manager was engrossed in her work. Suddenly the children let out a piercing scream. The manager rushed over to find them cowering at the bottom of the stairs leading to the balcony. The kids said that they saw a man standing at the top of the steps, looking down at them. When one of the theater's workers arrived, he asked the kids what the man looked like. They gave a very detailed description.

Days later, the same worker (we'll call him Greg) was closing up the theater, making sure that all the emergency exits were shut and locked. Going over to one of the last exits on his rounds, Greg chanced to look up at the projection booth and saw a man's head. Whoever it was quickly ducked away, but Greg got a good look at the face. It matched exactly the description given by the manager's children. The brave employee raced up to the projection room only to find no one there. There was only one way to get to the booth, and the worker had passed no one.

Shortly after this the Strand was sold. Upon meeting the new owner, Greg had a sense of deja vu. The new owner seemed strangely familiar. Apparently, the new owner's father had, at one time, owned the Strand. He had also committed suicide there...in the projection room.

To this day people report looking up at the projection room to see a man's face quickly duck away.

††††††††††††

Myths & Legends of Rochester

Rochester, Indiana, has had a rich and varied history since being settled in 1830. Elmo Lincoln, the silver screen's first Tarzan, was born there in 1889. The Cole Brothers-Clyde Beatty circus had their winter quarters there from 1935 until 1940. A fire in the buildings on February 20, 1940 resulted in elephants running down Main Street. Rochester was also the first stop on the Potawatomi Trail of Tears in 1838.

Eager to open up Northern Indiana for settlement, in 1836 the government signed an agreement with the Potawatomi called the Treaty of Yellow River. Under this agreement the tribe were given $1 per acre of their land and each member was granted a 320-acre parcel of land in Kansas. The Potowatomi were given two years to leave Indiana. Most did, but the Twin Lakes Village of Chief Menominee had to be forcibly removed. On August 30, 1838, General John Tipton and two hundred soldiers rounded up the remaining 859 natives. Once they were prepared for the journey, Tipton ordered the crops and their homes burned to discourage them from returning. The natives then began their long trek to Kansas. Their first stop to camp was just outside of Rochester, a twenty-one-mile journey. When the tribe made their way down Main Street on September 5th, they stretched from one end of town to the other. Many died before the last Potawatomi tribe could make it to Kansas.

The Prill School, located at Old Fort Wayne Road and 700 East, is part of the town's history. Built in 1876 on land donated by John Prill, the school was for all eight grades with students ranging in age between six and eighteen. One teacher taught them all in the one-room school. In the early days there was no plumbing in the building, so some of the older students carried water from the John Prill residence nearby. Older male students and the teacher also carried in wood to fire the wood-burning stove that sat in the middle of the room. Bag lunches were brought in by the students and kept in the cloakroom until noon. Often during the winter months, the food froze before lunchtime! The Prill School was the very model of a one-room schoolhouse. One can imagine pigtails being dunked into inkwells and other such shenanigans. The teacher kept order, though, using a long slender whip on the students when discipline was needed.

The school ceased operation in 1925. Shortly after that the windows were boarded up so that grain could be stored inside the building. When former student Dewey Zolman decided to restore the Prill School in 1971, he found all the windows broken out and old boards, grain, and farm equipment inside. With a lot of hard work and help from the community, the Prill School opened as a museum in time for the first Round Barn Festival that same year.

According to some, the renovations have brought back one of the former teachers. Sister Sarah now haunts the Prill School. The legend says that if you go out to the Prill School on the night of a full moon, you should park so that you can see the tree in the yard in your rearview mirror. Sister Sarah will then show herself, standing next to the tree. Also, if you leave a piece of paper with several questions on it by the tree, the following morning the questions will have the answers written in (after all, Sister Sarah was a teacher)! There are many tales, most of them conflicting, as to why Sister Sarah haunts the Prill School. One such story says that Sister Sarah's child is buried under the front steps of the school. Sounds of children inviting you to come play with them have also been heard.

The records don't show a Sarah listed as a teacher for the Prill School, but the names of several teachers are missing so it's possible Sarah did indeed once preside over students in the one-room schoolhouse.

Also in Rochester is a cemetery off of State Road 25 and 300 South. Some call this "Earl's Tree Cemetery." Ghost hunters visiting the graveyard with digital recorders don't hear anything at the time, but when reviewing the recorders later find EVPs. Among their normal conversations can be heard a whispered voice that is generally believed to be that of a three-year-old boy named Earl. Careful listeners can hear Earl talking about the tree next to his grave. Earl's ghost has also been seen, playing near the tree to which he seems so attached.

Chapter Fourteen
The Moody Lights

In the days of the horse and buggy, two brothers were traveling down Moody Road in Francesville when one of the brothers fell from the coach. He was decapitated as the rear wheel went over his body. The young man's head rolled off the road and into a cornfield. Legend says that his brother travels that road still, holding a ghostly lantern high, searching for his brother's head.

When the corn is high, the lantern light can be seen at the end of one of the rows of corn. If you watch, you can see the light slowly move down the row. When it gets to the end, the light pauses before turning to make its way down the next row of corn.

That's just one of the stories of the Moody lights.

TheShadowlands.net tells of another tale, one of a man appropriately named Moody who haunts the area. It is said that if you wait at Moody Road where the tree branches hang over the road you'll see him. He usually appears as a bright light coming right at you...

Edrick Thay found yet another story of the Moody lights. As reported in his book, *Ghost Stories of Indiana,* over a hundred years ago a farmer, not being of sound mind, did away with his daughter's suitor, a young man the farmer found undesirable. The farmer had tried everything from forbidding the two to meet to arranging for his daughter to meet other eligible young men. When none of these tactics worked, the farmer murdered his daughter's boyfriend. According to this tale, the Moody lights are the remnants of the ghost of a young man forever doomed to roam the countryside in search of his true love.

A similar story concerns a man who had been in the Mafia. Knowing he was sentenced for death from the mob, the man chose to hide out in the relative safety of a small Indiana town. The man stayed indoors most of the time, fearing that if he went out someone could recognize him and word would get out to the men who wanted him dead. The man had a daughter living with him, though, and she soon tired of staying home. On her birthday, she begged and pleaded with her father to be allowed to go out and party with her friends. He finally relented, but told her that on her return she should flash the car lights three times so that he would know it was her. This version says to see the Moody lights you must turn onto Moody Road and flash your lights three times. Then you drive to the end of the road and flash them three more times. At this, the spirit of the father will come out to meet you, dressed in an old robe and carrying a lantern. It is the light from this lantern that others, further off, see as the Moody lights.

Whatever the explanation, the Moody lights have fascinated folklore enthusiasts and ghost hunters for years.

Chapter Fifteen
The Lady in White
And Other Hammond Ghosts

The cab driver was having a slow night. Lost in his thoughts, he nearly didn't see the woman in white attempting to flag him down. The sight of her in his headlights jolted him back to reality. As he pulled over to the side of the road, he thought to himself that she was stunningly beautiful. A frown crossed his face as she pulled open the door and began to climb inside. The young woman was wearing a wedding dress.

Just why a lovely young bride was hailing a cab in the dead of night along Cline Avenue he couldn't fathom, but the cab driver told himself it wasn't his business. He looked back briefly to make sure she was safely inside. Whatever her reasons for being out so late, he could see the sorrow in her face. Quickly he turned back, keeping his face firmly forward. *A jilted bride,* he thought to himself. *Give her some space.* The last thing the driver needed that night was for some woman to suddenly become hysterical with grief in his cab.

In a neutral tone, he asked, "Where to?"

"Just drive." She spoke as if life no longer mattered.

The driver gave a small shrug and pulled the car back onto the road. He hadn't driven far, though, before he began to smell something odd. He could smell river water, and while they were close to the Calumet River all the windows of the cab were up. The smell grew stronger. Thinking he should check on his fare to see if the smell was bothering her as much as it was him, he looked into his rearview mirror. What he saw made him cry out in shock.

The young woman was sitting there in her wedding gown, but now the dress was soaked with water and horribly mud-stained. The woman's hair was matted and tangled and her face was the pale white of the dead. Her eyes stared ahead, unseeing.

Screaming, the driver nearly lost control of his vehicle. When he finally got the cab back straight on the road, he looked back. The woman was gone. The back seat was empty.

The cab driver just had an encounter with Hammond's *Lady in White*.

The ghost is said to be that of Sophia, a young Polish girl. In the days when Hammond was enjoying its first industrial boom many Polish families came to the area. Sophia, the only daughter of one such family, was a quiet, obedient girl, and quite devoted her parents. Many courted the beautiful Sophia, but the one she fell in love with was a 23-year-old boy of Puerto Rican descent. Knowing that her parents would never consent to such a match, Sophia met the young man in secret for many months. Their favorite spot to meet was just outside of town at a secluded area by the banks of Calumet River. Here their love grew, and soon they planned their wedding.

Sophia hated deceiving her parents, but she knew that if her father learned of her plans that he would forbid her to see the young man ever again, and that Sophia knew she could not do. Secretly she saved a little money every week. Sophia had her eyes set on a wedding gown she'd seen in a shop window in town. The young couple found a priest in Griffith who agreed to marry them, so the couple set a September date for their wedding.

On the day in question, Sophia told her parents that she would be working late. She took the money she'd saved and went to the store and purchased her gown. She then took a cab to Griffith, where she was to meet her beloved at the church.

The young man never showed.

Some say that he met with an accident at the mill where he worked. Others insist that he was rushing to the church and was killed in a car crash, and still others say that he simply got cold feet and realized that marriage wasn't for him. In any case, Sophia was left waiting at the church for hours.

Finally, the despondent girl took a cab and started for home. She had no idea how she would explain her actions to her parents, but she knew she had nowhere else to go. As the cab rolled down Cline Avenue it passed the spot where Sophia and her lover had spent so many hours planning their future. Suddenly the girl knew what she had to do. She yelled for the cabbie to stop his vehicle. The cab had barely come to a stop before Sophia had thrown open the door. As she ran towards the river the startled cab driver yelled at her to stop, but she seemed not to hear him. Sophia rushed into the water until the weight of her dress and the current pulled her under. Some fishermen found her body the following day.

Her ghost continues to be spotted by travelers on Cline Avenue as it nears Calumet River. Sometimes she's seen, forlorn and wet from the river, standing by the side of the road as if waiting for a ride. Occasionally fog and mist from the river will seem to form into a ghostly shape and appear right in front of an approaching vehicle. Other times people will see the Lady in White slowly disappearing into the river, once again to be swallowed up by the currents.

††††††††††††††

Bishop Noll Institute

Another haunted Hammond location, according to *Flashback,* a newsletter from the Hammond Historical Society, is the Bishop Noll Institute. This private school, a Catholic, coeducational junior/senior high school, boasts three separate spirits. Laughter can be heard from the old pool area, supposedly supplied by a freshman who drowned there. A janitor who hung himself on the second floor has been known to push chairs off desks during the night, and ghostly voices and footsteps are often heard here.

The school's auditorium is said to be haunted by the spirit of a young girl who hung herself from the catwalk. The story goes that she tried out for the lead in the school play. When she didn't get cast, she waited until the auditorium was empty and took her own life. Now, according to legend, those lucky enough to get the lead in the school play may not get to enjoy the experience. These young thespians have been known to lose their voices suddenly, become ill, or even fall off the stage!

Gavit High School

According to TheShadowlands.net, this high school has a ghost or two of its own. Around midnight, the sound of people walking on the roof can be heard. Windows that have been shut at night have been found open in the morning. Some have reported hearing muffled screams and even seen figures walking in the shadowy corridors. It seems like those who have had to work late and think that they're alone in the building may not be as alone as they thought.

Columbia Elementary School

A man living near Columbia Elementary School is said to still make his presence known years after his death. The man went through a very rough time, including a difficult divorce from his wife. He was denied visitation rights to his children and even lost his job. Mad with grief, the man hung himself. He can still be heard, though, trying to talk to neighbors as they go past his house. He's also been known to throw tools around his garage, making a huge racket. On the anniversary of his death, a white light can be seen in the windows of his home to remind the neighborhood of his tragic demise.

Ivanhoe, Indiana, Railroad Tracks

A tragic circus train accident in 1918 has spurred tales of a haunting that some say is still going on today. Just before 4 o'clock in the morning on June 22, an empty troop train rammed the Hagenbeck-Wallace Circus train. Of the three hundred circus performers and roadies aboard, eighty-six were killed and 127 injured. Many of the dead were burned beyond recognition.

The circus train was being pulled onto a side railing just beyond Hammond's eastern border at Ivanhoe, Indiana, to await being switched to the track that would take it into town. There the circus was to stop at the show grounds at Calumet Avenue and 150th Street to set their tents up for the day's festivities.

Unfortunately the troop train that was following missed several signals to stop as the engineer had dozed off. The troop train smashed into the circus train's caboose at nearly sixty miles an hour.

The flames from the resulting fire spread rapidly due to the kerosene lanterns that were used to light the sleeper cars of the circus train. In addition, many of the Pullman cars were made of wood. Rescue operations were also hindered by the large crowd that gathered to watch the tragedy. It was several days before all the bodies and the wreckage could be cleared away.

True to the adage that "the show must go on," the Hagenbeck-Wallace Circus only had to cancel one show, the one scheduled for Hammond. Borrowing acts and equipment from both Barnum and Bailey's and Ringling Brothers Circuses, Hagenbeck-Wallace continued their shows a mere two days later.

Many of the dead were buried in a section of Chicago's Woodlawn Cemetery called Showman's Rest. This area had only recently been set up by the Showman's League of America for just such an emergency. Since many of the dead were roustabouts who had only recently joined the circus, not all of the corpses could be identified. Several of the graves in Showman's Rest, therefore, are marked as Unknown Male or Unknown Female. Some have their nicknames or descriptions mark their final resting place, such as "Shorty," "Baldy," and even "4 Horse Driver."

A few years later five elephant statues were placed at Showman's Rest, one at each corner and one at the rear center of the plot. The elephants each have one leg raised with a ball underneath and their trunks are lowered to symbolize mourning.

Perhaps because of the elephant statues, a story has sprung up that elephants and other circus animals are also buried at Showman's Rest. Some have even suggested that the elephants died while heroically trying to pull circus performers free from the wreckage. Indeed, at the site of the wreck one is supposed to be able to sometimes hear the screams of the animals as they burned to death.

Records show, however, that not a single animal died in the train wreck.

If people are really hearing ghostly screams at the site, they obviously aren't coming from spectral elephants. Maybe what's being carried in the wind on certain nights are the dying screams of the eighty-six men and women who perished...

Chapter Sixteen
More than a Home

The Speakeasy

There was, in those dim days of the past, a tavern located in the southwest neighborhood of Gary called Black Oak. While the two-story structure is no longer standing, the memory of the place—and the ghosts associated with it—lingers on.

During prohibition, the tavern was a notorious speakeasy. Run by extremely shady characters, the bar offered not only bootleg liquor, but also gambling and ladies of the evening. Many violent acts took place within its walls, including robbery, rape, and murder. Fights broke out quite frequently, and it's also likely that the owners from this time met with a violent end.

The building remained empty for many years and it's during this period that the tavern's reputation for being haunted flourished. A strange re-enactment of one particular night seemed to periodically play itself out, frightening any unwary visitor unlucky enough to wander through the darkened tavern after sundown.

More than one person has witnessed this ghostly performance from the past. It would begin with the sound of a car pulling up to the side of the building. Doors would then slam, and footsteps would be heard going to the basement door, followed by a rapid knocking. There would be a short pause after hearing the basement door open...before the loud retort of gunshots filled the air.

One can easily imagine what must have happened back in those dangerous days of bootleggers, G-Men, and crime syndicates. The owner in some way must have been holding out on his bosses and hitmen arrived to remedy the situation. The sounds of the shooting continued to replay years after the event, heard by those that dared to spend the night in the abandoned tavern.

The phenomenon was not only auditory, however. Several people claim to have seen the ghost of the owner rushing up the stairs from the basement. The phantom was even known to shove people out of his way in his haste to escape his fate.

One of the women of ill-repute has also been seen. Always appearing in a long red dress, the woman had been reported to look straight at people, beckoning them to come closer.

The tavern has long since been torn down, and one would think that put an end to the ghostly activity. This is not the case. The woman in the red dress still haunts the land where the tavern once stood. She still beckons to those unlucky enough to see her—an invitation one should steadfastly refuse.

The Kaske House

A tavern built by David Gibson in 1837 originally dominated the property. This was taken over by the Brass family in 1845 and remodeled into a large, two-story inn that they called the Brass Tavern. The town of Munster was non-existent at the time (Munster wasn't incorporated until 1907), so the Brass Tavern served mainly as a stagecoach stop and a place for local farmers to gather.

The inn was eventually sold to Johann and Wilhelmina Stallbohm. The Stallbohm Inn, as it was now known, continued to operate until the 1890s. After closing the Inn, the Stallbohms continued to live there. Upon the deaths of Johann and Wilhelmina, daughter Wilhelmina inherited the house and she and her husband Hugo Kaske moved back from Minneapolis to remodel the place. On Halloween night in 1909 a fire broke out after a party. The family managed to escape unharmed, but the house was destroyed. They rebuilt it in 1910, putting their new home further back on the lot.

Helen Bieker, Wilhelmina's daughter, inherited the house upon Wilhelmina's death.

In 1968 Helen sold several acres of the land to the Munster Board of Parks and Recreation. The remaining acres of family property were sold to the Parks Board in 1986 with the understanding that Helen would live there for her remaining days. She died two years later. Today the house is run as a museum.

It's also known to be haunted.

A woman dressed in white has been seen in the windows, day or night, gazing out at the landscape. People believe she is the ghost of Wilhelmina Kaske. Inside the house, strange knocking sounds have been heard and chandeliers have been known to swing on their own. One famous story concerns a painter who was working on restoring the house. He was intending to paint over Wilhelmina's favorite wallpaper. He didn't get very far, for after a few strokes his can of paint flew at him. Soaked with paint, he fled the building.

Other ghosts have been spotted at the Kaske house. Around the gazebo, a young couple has been seen holding hands. They walk silently around the gazebo before vanishing into thin air.

The Kaske family was proud of their house and grounds. No one wanted to see the area developed for commercial purposes. It seems some family members have stayed on to ensure their wishes are kept.

The Inn at Aberdeen

She's often been seen standing at the foot of the stairs, looking very sweet and innocent. Sometimes she's been known to wander down the hall or visit people in their rooms. In her more mischievous moods she's been

118 More than a Home: The Inn at Aberdeen

known to move things around in the guests' rooms... *She's also vanished right before people's eyes.*

And people who stay at the Inn at Aberdeen say the ghost looks amazingly like the girl in the framed lithograph at the top of the stairs.

Courtesy of the Inn at Aberdeen.

     The Inn at Aberdeen, located in Valparaiso, is a beautiful old farmhouse that now serves as an eleven-suite bed and breakfast. Originally called Timberlake Farm, records show that the home goes back at least to 1856. It was the home of John Ritter (no relation to the actor John Ritter) and his family in the late 1800s. A photograph of the family now graces the Old Entry to the Inn, showing the house as it looked then. Over the years it has been a dairy farm and a thoroughbred horse farm. Today, the Inn at Aberdeen is a popular and award-winning retreat, a great place for business meetings or just to get away. Many weddings and receptions have been held there. The Inn was picked as the best retreat center for meetings by *Indiana Business Magazine*.

It is also haunted.

When John Johnson bought the old Ritter house in the fall of 1994, he knew he could transform it into a bed and breakfast. He didn't know that he was acquiring a ghost as well. When John and his wife Linda opened the Inn for business in December of 1995, they placed a diary in each of the rooms so that guests could write about their experiences. They thought that it would be fun for people to write about spending their wedding night at the Inn, having a special celebration, or things of that nature. It wasn't long before the Johnsons began seeing entries about a ghostly little girl. Interestingly, the sightings were being written about in quite a few of the diaries, so it wasn't just a case of one person writing about a ghost and then other people staying in that same room continuing on with the legend. Nearly all the diaries contained encounters of some sort, written by guests who wouldn't have seen the other diaries.

There have been no violent deaths at the inn. The farm's history bears no suicides or murders, though several deaths have occurred there over the years, including Sara Ritter and at least two children, either by accidents or natural causes. The 150-year-old Inn may have been part of the Underground Railroad, but nothing horrific is known to have happened there.

So who is the little girl who haunts the Inn? One theory, suggested by Wanda Lou Willis in her book *More Haunted Hoosier Trails,* is that it isn't the Inn that's haunted—it's the lithograph by E. C. Barnes that graces the wall at the top of the stairs. Haunted paintings and lithographs aren't uncommon. Many a haunting centers around a certain object, such as a painting, and often when the object moves to a different home, so does the ghost. One can even find haunted paintings being sold on eBay!

E. C. Barnes specialized in lithographs, mainly of Victorian children. The picture over the stairs at the Inn at Aberdeen shows the little girl in a long nightgown, holding a kitten in her arms. At her feet is a puppy. She's the very essence of purity and innocence...a Dickensian character just like the ghost that people swear they've seen at the Inn.

Extensive remodeling has been known to stir up paranormal activity, and certainly the Johnsons had to change quite a lot to transform the old home into a functional bed and breakfast. There was work done in the 1930s and 40s to add a second story to the north end of the house and indoor plumbing, but the Johnsons worked hard to keep the integrity of the original home while creating a safe, comfortable, and functional environment for their guests. The ventilating, heating, and plumbing systems all had to be replaced. The Bristol Solarium was added. Walls were demolished and new rooms added. While the work was being done, a trap door was found in one of the closets that led to the old root cellar. A crawlspace also went under the living room, leading some to believe the house had been used as part of the Underground Railroad. While there are no historic records to show this was the case, it certainly is possible the home could have been used as a way station from a known Underground Railroad location in Hebron to other sites further north.

Other paranormal activity has occurred at the Inn. One guest, who had the door to her room locked and bolted, arranged her jewelry on the dresser in preparation for getting ready for a night out. On coming out of the bathroom, she found that several items were missing and the rest were in disarray. She checked the door, but it was still bolted so she knew no one could have entered. Puzzled, she returned to the bathroom to finish dressing. When she came back out, the missing jewelry was back and everything was perfectly in place. The woman concluded that the mischievous ghost had simply been playing with her.

The Aberdeen Suite seems especially active. Here, along with cold spots and shifting items, the gas fireplace has been known to come on all by itself. Guests have been sleeping peacefully only to be awakened by having the fire suddenly roar into life. Two of the cleaning staff experienced the same phenomenon while working in the Aberdeen Suite. Johnson has had a workman out to inspect the fireplace, but was told that it's in perfect working order and impossible for the fire to start on its own.

One odd occurrence happened to a friend of Johnson's, who was helping out at the Inn. Working the front desk, he saw a young woman enter with a young girl. The two went into the solarium and sat. Johnson's friend thought nothing about this, as guests often sit in the solarium while their car is being parked and other family members are gathering bags. He did take note, however, when the girl, who he guessed at being around eleven years of age, began to talk about the house and its history in a very knowledgeable way. She even knew about the trap door in the closet. The girl chatted on, telling her mother all about the house until suddenly the conversation stopped and the two went back outside. The desk clerk, puzzled, went after them to see if he could help out in any way. He found no one there. There were no cars in the parking lot. The young woman and the little girl had seemingly vanished.

John Johnson isn't sure that he believes in the ghost stories. He was curious enough, however, to allow Indiana Ghost Trackers to conduct an investigation. Armed with cameras, EMF detectors, and audio recorders, the Ghost Trackers came to the Inn in April of 2002. They had quite an evening.

Touring the house, the team didn't get anything on film or their voice recorders in the Aberdeen Suite, but the *EMF detectors* — devices that detect electro-magnetic fields, which some paranormal investigators believe can help locate spirits — did detect some unusual energy levels. As they were leaving the room, the door opened about six inches on its own. They checked the door and could find no reason why it should move on its own. Again as they left, the door opened as if someone was peeking out at them. The Ghost Trackers also had psychic impressions of a little girl's presence in the old basement. Their voice recorders also picked up an EVP in this area. In response to a question by one of the investigators, a voice can be heard on the recording saying, "We're here. You're beautiful." The voice couldn't be heard at the time, but was very clear upon playback of the tape.

The Ghost Trackers left with the feeling that the Inn has at least two ghosts, the little girl and another ghost, a male that seems to prefer the basement. The reason the ghosts haunt the Inn, however, remains a mystery.

Ghost Hunter Robert Davis of Robs Ghost Team also investigated the Inn. During his stay, Davis felt cold spots on the staircase leading up to the second floor. He also felt as if someone was watching him in the Aberdeen Suite. While trying to catch a few hours of sleep in his room, the Alloway Suite, Davis was awakened by the sound of footsteps outside in the hallway. Quickly rising and rushing to the door, Davis found the corridor empty. There was no sign that anyone was up and about...*no one flesh and bone, anyway*.

You can't go wrong in picking the Inn at Aberdeen for a stay. Johnson, being a perfect host, is happy to accommodate his guest's wishes: "If they want a chance to see the ghost, I'll put them in the old part of the house, where there's been the most activity reported. If they want nothing to do with ghosts, I'll steer them clear of those areas!"

Courtesy of the Inn at Aberdeen.

Chapter Seventeen
The House of Evil

The following story was told to me by a young woman named Cassandra. She and the remaining members of her family attest to the truthfulness of these events. To protect their identities, the exact location of the house in question isn't given and some names have been changed. Cassandra was just a young girl at the time of these events, but she and her brother and sister still occasionally talk about the terror they experienced. Even now, remembering the past brings a shiver up their spines...

†††††††††

Jeffrey knew what he had to do and where it had to be done. The garage, of course. The garage was where Jeffrey had spent so many hours, sometimes working on one project or another, sometimes just sitting in the quiet, thinking. At one time the garage had been a refuge, a place to get away from the house. That hadn't worked, of course. The house was too powerful, too strong. It could reach out and mentally grab you no matter where you hid. There was only one way to defeat the house.

Jeffrey carefully closed the door behind him. The sound of the closure, wood banging on wood, echoed for a moment in the rafters. Then...*all* was silent. Jeffrey enjoyed the quiet, smiling to himself. He ambled slowly over to the workbench, admiring the tools there. There was still so much work that needed to be done. The house was old, but in pretty good condition. Still, repairs needed to be done. Now they would just have to be done by someone else.

Slowly, Jeffrey brought the gun up to his head. Opening his mouth, he steadied himself. It would all be over in a matter of moments, and he would be at peace. The house would no longer have its hold over him.

The loud bang shattered the stillness of the day as blood splattered against the wall. Jeffrey fell to the floor, finally at peace.

†††††††††

Alice felt more than slightly uneasy moving her family into their new home on Old Porter Road. After all, it hadn't been too long ago that Uncle Jeffrey had taken his own life in what was now their garage. It would be impossible not to think of that every time the garage even came into view, at least for a while. Aunt Jane wouldn't be helping them settle in, either. That was for sure. Jane was reluctant to even set foot back inside the house, and who could blame her? According to Jane, Jeffrey hadn't been himself for months prior to his suicide, spending a large part of his time in the garage.

Alice hoped that the presence of a new family, one with two young girls and a boy, would bring happiness to the house. Houses seemed to hold on to tragedy, giving them a slightly off-kilter feel and this one had seen its share of death. Long before Jeffrey killed himself, a previous owners had died of a heart attack in one of the upstairs bedrooms. There were probably others that Alice didn't even know about. After all, the house *was* old.

And in need of repair.

She and her husband, Brian, had agreed, when they took over renting the property, to continue the repair work started by Jeffrey. First, though, she had to get their new home organized. There were dozens of boxes to unload and rooms to decorate as best she could. There was the living room, kitchen, bathroom, and one bedroom downstairs, and upstairs there were three more bedrooms, another living room, a bathroom, and a huge storage closet. It was, Alice knew, going to take a lot of work...almost as much work as forgetting what had happened in the garage.

Weeks later, Alice was enjoying a quiet evening on her own. Brian was outside in the garage, working on yet another project. How he could spend so much time out there, standing and working in practically the same spot where Jeffrey had killed himself? Alice didn't know. At least the kids were sleeping soundly. Charlie, Cassie, and Lisa had, after their usual struggle, gone to bed fairly quickly. They would by now be dreaming sweet dreams.

As she walked down the hall, Alice realized that one of her children had yet to drift off. She could hear Cassie's small voice coming from her room. It was a faint sound, but it seemed to Alice as if her daughter was deep in conversation with someone.

Alice softly rapped on her daughter's door. "Cassandra? Are you okay?"

There was a short pause. "Yes."

Alice opened the door. Inside, Cassandra was sitting up in bed. Her bedside lamp was on, casting huge shadows across the room. "I thought I heard you talking with someone," Alice said quietly. Next door, Charlie would be sleeping soundly and she didn't want to disturb him.

"I was," came Cassie's reply. "I was talking with my friend."

Alice smiled. She was used to imaginary friends. All children seemed to have one at some time or another. "Well, tell your friend that it's time to go to bed. You can talk to each other in the morning."

Cassandra looked uncertain, but she nodded. "Alright," she said. She leaned over to switch off her bedside light.

As the room was plunged into darkness, Alice felt goose pimples rise on her arms. It seemed, just for a second, that there was someone else in the room beside Cassie and herself. She shook the thought away. "Goodnight, sweetheart," she said.

The odd occurrences kept coming. In the following weeks Alice had, at different times, found each of her children seemingly talking to an invisible entity. She supposed it could just be that each of her children had conjured up an imaginary playmate to deal with the stress of moving to a new place, but somehow she didn't think this was the case. And then there was Brian, who seemed to be spending all of his free time in the garage. Granted, they had agreed to continue the repairs to the house, but Brian seemed obsessed with the garage, often staying out there until late at night. When she asked him what he was doing out there, he would growl at her, telling her that he was working and if she didn't like it...

It wasn't like Brian. Not at all. He didn't seem to be getting enough sleep. There were dark circles under his eyes and he seemed to be walking slower than his normal step.

Alice was nearly asleep one night when she realized that Brian had come into the bedroom. She was a little surprised, as lately he generally didn't come to bed until she was fast asleep. She listened as he stripped off his clothes in the dark and slipped into bed. "Goodnight," he said, his tone a little curt.

"Goodnight." Alice pulled her covers tighter around her and willed herself to get some sleep.

She wasn't sure if she'd actually nodded off or if Brian's cries had awakened her. Alice only knew that her husband was now sitting bolt upright in bed. She could feel the tension coming off of him in waves and in the moonlight from the window she could see that his eyes were wide open and staring at the door.

"What is it?" she asked worriedly. "What's wrong?"

Brian's words came out in a growl. "Tim's in the house again."

Alice thought she heard wrong. As Brian brushed the covers aside and got out of bed, she asked with a frown, "Tim? Who's Tim?"

Her husband was moving for the door. "Tim," he answered, as if that was all the information she needed.

Alarmed, Alice followed Brian out into the hall. "Who's Tim?" she asked again.

Brian was moving quickly, his anger apparent in both his movements and his voice. "Get out of here! You're not wanted!" He seemed, to Alice, to be bellowing at the air.

"Honey, there's no one there," she said. "You must have been dreaming." She was aware of a shuffling sound behind her. Turning, she saw her daughter Lisa, eyes still heavy from sleep, coming down the hall towards her.

"What's going on?" Lisa asked, her voice shaking a little.

"Nothing. Go on back to sleep," Alice told her.

By now Brian had gone downstairs. Alice could see him standing in the darkness of the living room, his shoulders bunched as if ready for a fight.

"Get out!" he shouted. "You're not wanted here! Get out of this house!"

It took Alice some time to calm her husband down. When he finally became more rational, he refused to answer her questions about who Tim might be. He just wanted to go back to sleep, he told her.

He didn't want to come back to the bedroom. He slept the rest of the night on the couch in the upstairs living room.

Brian continued to spend his nights on the couch. When he wasn't at work, he spent most of his time in the garage, only coming in when exhaustion forced him to agree to a few hours rest. "Tim," whoever or whatever Tim was, seemed to plague him. Several nights Brian awoke and would shout at this unseen person, chasing him out of the house.

Brian wasn't alone in seeing phantoms. The children talked about "the earring lady," a woman they saw several times around the house. Whenever they spotted her, the woman was always in the process of putting on her earrings. They also continued to have conversations with their invisible friends, although Alice was beginning to wonder if there was something more to this as well.

Other weird things began to happen. Laundry baskets that were taken upstairs would disappear only to be found back downstairs. The first time this happened, Alice told herself that she only *thought* she'd brought the basket upstairs, but it happened too often to be mere forgetfulness. Food would fly off the kitchen table. Something could be at the center of the table and in seconds it would be on the floor. When it happened it wasn't like the item—a banana, a box of cereal, whatever—rolled or was pushed off. The thing would lift off the table and seemed to throw itself to the floor.

Then Charlie refused to sleep in the downstairs bedroom any longer. When Alice asked him why, he was reluctant at first to say. After some coaxing, Charlie admitted it was because of the lady.

"What lady?" Alice asked.

"She sits on the cabinets and looks into my room," the boy replied. "She scares me."

A chill went down Alice's spine. She hugged her boy close to her. "We'll work something out," she said. "You won't have to sleep in that room anymore."

Brian switched to the night shift at work. Alice knew that he did so to be away from the house at night, but if he had thought that would bring an end to his troubles, he'd been mistaken. He still kept mostly to the garage, and if the kids came around when the door was closed he yelled at them. Occasionally he still saw "Tim," even though Alice assured him that there was no such person. She even asked the neighbors, and no one could recall a Tim ever living in the house.

The kids still conversed with their unseen pals as well, although Alice wasn't sure they were unseen by the children. She seemed to be the only one that couldn't see the phantoms of their home. Once, when she came upon Cassandra chatting with one of her "friends," Alice asked her daughter to tell her what her companion looked like. Her daughter looked up at her angrily. "You're scaring my friends away," she said.

Alice knew things couldn't go on like this. Something had to give.

And soon, it did.

Brian was getting ready for work and seemed in even more of a foul mood than usual. They were in the downstairs living room, and Alice's apprehension rose as she watched her husband stomp around the room, muttering to himself. She couldn't hear everything he was saying, but the name Tim came up several times. There was something in Brian's eyes that frightened Alice, and she wanted him out of the house before he exploded. Cassandra was the only other one in the house as Charlie was still at school and Lisa was visiting Grandma. "Shouldn't you be getting to work?" she asked.

He paused to glare at her. "I know what's going on."

"What's going on? What are you talking about?"

"Tim's told me everything. I know what the two of you have been doing behind my back."

Alice's heart seemed to stop beating. She had to force herself to draw in a breath. "Honey, there is no Tim. I don't know any Tim. Whatever you've heard, it isn't..."

Brian advanced on her threateningly. "Don't you lie to me!" he bellowed.

"I'm not..." Alice's words were cut off as Brian clamped his hands around her throat. She tried to struggle, but the strength of his grip quickly sapped her energy. She heard an odd sound and realized it was her own strangled cry. As the room started to dim, Alice could hear her daughter Cassandra scream. The girl must have heard the commotion and had come to investigate. Out of the corner of her eye Alice saw Cassie going over to the phone on the table by the couch.

Brian saw her as well. He let go of Alice's throat and was over to the phone in a second. Before Cassandra could dial the first number, he ripped the phone cord out of the wall. Then the shoved the child aside, sending her sprawling to the floor.

Everything seemed to freeze. Alice, tears streaming down her face, realized that Brian was standing immobile, his shoulders hunched. She rubbed her throat and went over to help Cassandra get back to her feet.

She knew that, no matter what, there was no way that she or her children were going to spend another night in that house. She and Cassie would pick Charlie up from school and then they would stay at Grandma's house or a hotel—ANYWHERE BUT THIS HOUSE.

Without a word, she took her daughter and headed for the door.

Cassandra remembers spending the next several nights at hotels and at her Grandmother's. A week later, her mother took her, Charlie and Lisa back to the house on Old Porter Road to gather up their things.

Her mother was obviously nervous as she pulled into the driveway. Their dad's car was there, and Cassandra saw her mother's face tighten as she parked behind it.

The kids followed their mother inside. They found their father seated at the kitchen table, smoking a cigarette. He looked calm but haggard. Cassandra recalls that his eyes were red and that his face was unnaturally pale. Slowly, he looked up at his family as they stood in the doorway.

"We've got to get out of here," he said simply.

Alice and Brian convinced the landlord to break their lease.

The landlord and his wife took up residency in the house on Old Porter Road. They owned both that house and the one next door, which was in poor condition. Years later, Alice ran into the landlord's wife and asked how things were. The landlord's wife complained that her husband seemed obsessed with the house next door, spending nearly all of his waking hours over there working. There had also been some odd things that had happened at their house, things which the landlord's wife had no explanation for...

The house is still there, although it has gone through several renovations since Cassandra and her family lived there. Her dad won't talk about their time there. Whenever somebody mentions that house, he changes the subject. Cassandra isn't entirely sure what exactly was going on during their time on Old Porter Road, but she knows she wouldn't set foot across the threshold again for any amount of money.

She and her siblings still talk about that time, though. Their mother passed away several years ago, but to her dying day she never blamed her husband for his actions during that time. It had been the house, she maintained, that made him behave that way.

Cassandra knows that something evil lived with them in that house. And she suspects that the evil still lurks there, waiting to claim its next victim...

Author's Note: All names in the preceding story have been changed. While I have dramatized the story, the person who reported the events ("Cassandra") attests to the truthfulness of what happened in the house on Old Porter Road.

Chapter Eighteen
Diana of the Dunes

Some say she lives there still, wandering the Indiana Dunes that she loved so much. Visitors to the state park have spotted her running nude along the shores of Lake Michigan or taking a moonlight swim in the cold waters. She is possibly Indiana's most famous ghost.

The woman who would later be more widely known as Diana of the Dunes was born Alice Mable Gray in Chicago in 1881. She came from a well-to-do family, her father being a prominent physician. At the age of 16 she enrolled at the University of Chicago, where she studied astronomy, mathematics, Latin and Greek. An excellent student, Gray was a Phi Beta Kappa honor society member.

After graduating in 1903, Gray traveled to Germany, where she continued her studies at the University of Gottinger. It was there that Gray learned about a movement called Wandervogel, or Birds of Passing. This movement encouraged young people to give up their worldly possessions and to live in nature. This and a love of Lord Byron's poem "Solitude" would later cause Gray to her try her hand at the solitary life.

Gray returned to Chicago and began work at an astronomy magazine. Reports differ as to her actual position at the magazine, varying from secretary to associate editor. Whatever her position, Gray grew to hate the daily office grind, later referring to it as "slavery."

In 1915 the 34-year-old Gray left her job and her family and headed for the Indiana Dunes. Many reasons have been given for Gray's decision to abandon her city life. Some have said that an unhappy love affair drove her to a more secluded life while others maintain that her deteriorating eyesight made working at the magazine difficult. More likely it had always been her dream to live simply on the land and she finally decided to live out that dream, taking the next train out of Chicago.

Gray came to the Dunes, a place where she remembered having so many wonderful vacations as a child. She loved the area with its stark beauty. According to an interview she gave to the *Chicago Examiner* less than a year later, she arrived with few possessions and no real plan. Her first four nights were spent under the stars until she came across an abandoned fisherman's shack. This she made her home. "Then I began housekeeping," she later said, "and all the furniture I have is made of driftwood. Everything is driftwood here, including myself, and I have named the place 'Driftwood.'"

While she kept mostly to herself, she was by no means the hermit some accounts have made her out to be. She went into town often to get a few supplies and to borrow books from the library. She was even known to give tours of the Dunes to children.

Local fishermen began to catch sight of a nude woman swimming by the shore. The tales of Alice Gray's occasional nakedness soon made her a local legend. Before long reporters came to seek out the "water nymph" to get her story. Gray probably granted interviews with the notion of setting the record straight in an attempt to downplay her notoriety, but the reporters only fueled the fire. They downplayed Alice's education and most of what she told them, preferring to paint a different picture. They portrayed Alice as the goddess Diana, running nude and living free.

Their descriptions were flowery, depicting her as an unusually beautiful young woman with long, flowing raven tresses. Diana, they reported, could often be seen slipping into the cold waters of Lake Michigan without a stitch on her. Instead of stopping the local gossip as Gray must have wished, she now became even more of a legend. Now she was a 'goddess' of the Dunes.

These depictions of Gray were hardly accurate. In her middle thirties, Gray could hardly be described as young, and if photographs of her from the time are any indication she was hardly a tall, raven-haired beauty. Alice Gray was rather short and somewhat nondescript, but that description didn't sell newspapers.

While most of those who met Alice Gray knew her to be quiet and shy, her notoriety began to cause her problems. The fishermen of the area began to find excuses to linger around the beaches where Gray swam naked. As reported by Beth Scott and Michael Norman in their book *Haunted Heartland*, one fisherman's wife became furious over her husband's obsession with Diana of the Dunes. She angrily went to Gray's shack only to be warned away by the recluse, who was armed with a gun and had a wild dog by her side.

Gray was an early advocate for making the Dunes a National Park. The *Chesterton Tribune* of April 5, 1917 had an article proclaiming that Diana of the Dunes would be among those making a speech at the Great Dunes Pageant being held in Chicago's Fullerton Hall. The Dunes did later become a State Park in 1923 and decades later was established as a National Park.

In 1920 a man entered Gray's life. Paul Wilson had a mysterious past. He claimed to be an out-of-work boat builder, and while that may be true some sources believe that he had a prison record and that at one time he went by a different name. At first the couple were happy, with Paul helping out by catching fish and making and selling furniture. Wilson, known to possess a fierce temper, also kept reporters away from the woman now known more as Diana than by her real name.

Tragedy struck when a body was found on the beach close to Gray's hut in June of 1922. The unidentified man was beaten and strangled and then partially burned. Hikers came across the grisly remains and immediately alerted the authorities. Unpopular with the locals, Paul Wilson was the chief suspect. Eugene Frank, a deputy hired to look after the dunes cottages, went to Gray's to confront Wilson. A fight broke out, during which Gray was hit on the side of the head with Frank's gun and Wilson was shot in the foot.

Gray's skull was fractured and she was transported to a hospital in Gary. Both Frank and Wilson were taken into custody.

While Alice Gray lay near death in her hospital bed, her relatives went to her home and removed her books and manuscripts. Believing Gray wouldn't recover from her injuries, they wanted to preserve the material.

Meanwhile, Paul Wilson, sitting in his jail cell, claimed that the killer was actually an insane hermit named Burke. He described Burke as a gun-toting madman who walked with a pronounced limp and stated that he'd seen Burke's unmistakable footprints by the body. No sign of any such hermit could be found, and of course by then any footprints were long since gone. The body on the beach was never identified and Wilson was eventually released, there not being enough evidence to connect him with the murder.

Gray left the hospital, but never really recovered from her injuries. The couple briefly returned to their shack on the Dunes, but a new development called Ogden Dunes was being built right in their area. Dispossessed, the couple moved to Texas for a year. Gray grew homesick, though, and the couple came back and moved to Michigan City, where Wilson sold furniture. Still sickly after her brain injuries, Gray contracted uremic poisoning and died in Wilson's arms on February 11, 1925. She was buried in Gary's Oak Lawn Cemetery, despite her wish to be cremated and her ashes scattered across the dunes.

Later evidence showed that her life with Wilson might not have been a happy one. While she did indeed die of uremic poisoning, the bruises on her back and abdomen showed that she'd been beaten severely. Wilson himself ended up in a California prison. After his release he was shot to death while in the act of stealing a car.

Haunted Heartland, by Beth Scott and Michael Norman, revealed that the legend of Diana of the Dunes was far from over. It was discovered that Alice Gray was buried in a plot with several other bodies. Even in death she could not find the solitude she sought in life.

But Alice Gray, or Diana, has been seen after death. The ghost of a nude woman running along the beach has been spotted many times, and campers have spotted a solitary swimmer who suddenly vanishes on moonlit nights. Alice has been immortalized in another way as well. Every year the Diana of the Dunes Festival is held to honor one of northern Indiana's most famous legends.

Chapter Nineteen
Big City Haunts

Haunted Huntington

Huntington, known as "Lime City," is the largest city in Huntington County. As well as being the county seat, Huntington also has some interesting ghostly legends.

A popular and informative attraction, the Forks of the Wabash preserves that uneasy time in Indiana history when the first permanent white settlers began to arrive and mingled with the Indians still living in the area. At the Forks of the Wabash, visitors can check out a pioneer schoolhouse and the Nuck Log House. A visit to "the Chief's House," the Miami's council house, may not only prove educational but could bring one face-to-face with a ghost.

Chief Jean Baptiste Richardville, whose Miami name Peshewa meant "the wildcat," had the council house built at the Forks in 1834. Several treaty negotiations were held on the grounds of the house, which was also used for the council meetings of the Miami tribe. When Francis Lafontaine (or Topeah, meaning "frost on the bushes," if we go by his Miami name) succeeded Richardville in the early 1840s, he made the building his main residence. Today the house is preserved as it would have been in 1846, the last year Lafontaine lived there. It is possible that some of the residents from that time also remain.

There is a spot in the old servant's quarters that is known as "the pillar of ice." Visitors have reported that crossing this spot is like being hit by an icy cold breeze. Phantom voices have also been heard throughout the house. A man and a woman have also been spotted at the Chief's House. This couple, sometimes seen together and sometimes separately, has been known to vanish before the astonished eyes of visitors.

Huntington College is said to be haunted by the ghost of a woman who is always seen wearing a long white dress. She haunts the hallways of the Physical Education Recreation Center and for some reason only men can see her floating figure. The showers and lights here have also been known to turn on and off by themselves.

A fun urban legend tells of a woman who was killed on a train track near Polk Street. One version of this tale has her searching for her dropped wedding ring by the side of the tracks when she was struck by an oncoming freight train. One can only imagine how engrossed she must have been in her search not to hear the train approach! A more likely account tells us she was simply trying to beat the oncoming train in her car and misjudged the timing, resulting in a very bloody crash.

The legend warns that going over these tracks around 3 o'clock in the morning may cause your car to stall. If it dies, the phantom woman will obligingly push the car off the tracks. Her spirit will then float into the car and she will enter the mind of one of the car's occupants. This person will then get to see the woman's final moments and feel her death agonies.

It has been suggested that, as Polk doesn't cross any railroad tracks, that the crossing in question is actually on North Lafontaine, which connects to Polk Street. Others maintain that, in typical urban legend fashion, things have become garbled in the re-telling of the tale and that the tracks involved actually cross Pook Road, located east of nearby South Whitley.

In any case, having the woman's thoughts thrust into one's head isn't the end of the story. After leaving the tracks, one would be wise to carefully examine the trunk of the car. The bloody handprints of the ghost may be seen where the woman shoved the car off of the tracks!

†††††††††††††

The Ghosts of Fort Wayne

The second largest city in Indiana, Fort Wayne was named after United States General and American Revolutionary War statesman "Mad" Anthony Wayne. There are those that claim that much of Fort Wayne was built over Indian burial grounds, which may explain why specters seems to be around every corner in this Allen County city.

On Coldwater Street, a popular retail store is haunted by a man fond of playing Scottish tunes on the bagpipes. Sources say that around 3 o'clock in the morning the faint sounds of bagpipe music can often be heard. Soon after the music ceases, the man himself, wearing a green plaid kilt, is seen walking down the aisles. Witnesses claim to feel a cold, eerie feeling as he passes. The piper is a friendly ghost apparently, so if you spot him be sure to smile and give him a wave. Maybe he's just waiting for someone to request "*Danny Boy.*"

The old Mason Long house on Columbia Street still houses Long's spirit. Long, a notorious nineteenth century gambler and rogue, suddenly gave up his wanton ways and began to live a quiet life. He wrote books denouncing his former lifestyle (one popular title was *Save the Ladies*) and lectured extensively. Perhaps Mason Long feels he had unfinished business on this Earth and that's why his spirit still roams the house he once lived in.

The Embassy Theatre is so popular among both staff and patrons that some don't like to leave, even after death has claimed them. One maintenance man in particular still makes his ghostly rounds and has been spotted often.

The old Lutheran Hospital on Fairfield had a haunted fourth floor. The ghost of a man who died there was known to walk down the corridor, looking in different rooms as if searching for someone. The hospital has since been torn down.

Several bridges in Fort Wayne have a reputation for being haunted.

Bostick Road Bridge, which runs over St. Mary's River, is no longer in use for automobile traffic. Through the years, the bridge has been rumored to be a gathering place for satanic rituals, and many sacrifices are said to have taken place there. Perhaps that's why witnesses have claimed to been chased by strange animals in the woods near the bridge. People brave enough to check out Bostick Bridge at night have reported that at times the entire bridge shakes alarmingly. The bridge may be old, having been erected in 1894 according to a plaque affixed at the top of the bridge, but only the strongest of winds would cause the whole structure to shake. Besides, the shaking has occurred on nights when there was no wind. Bright orange shapes have been seen around the bridge, and glowing eyes have been seen in the nearby trees. One witness claimed to have found over a dozen mutilated squirrels by the bridge. The animals were placed in a stack, their heads having been apparently bitten off.

Bostick Bridge.

Another haunted bridge can be found just west of Van Buren Street. A woman in a long white dress haunts Main Street Bridge. The tale starts in the 1880s, when people downtown witnessed this woman rushing down Main Street to the bridge. They saw her reach the middle of the bridge and then...*vanish*. Fearing she had thrown herself over the side in a suicide attempt, the witnesses alerted the police. A search followed, but no sign of the woman or her body could be found.

A week later, the scene replayed itself. The woman was seen to run to the middle of the bridge only to disappear from sight.

Not long after this the woman in the white dress was seen again, this time riding in a horse-drawn carriage. The carriage sped down Main Street and again vanished when reaching the middle of the bridge.

Main Street Bridge.

The police, tired of being called in to find a woman who seemed to vanish at will, decided that they would be ready next time and waited by the bridge for the woman to appear. When she did, an officer approached her. The woman took off running and led the police on a chase that ended in an alley off College Street. Here the officers cornered the woman and threw a blanket over her. The blanket fell to the ground, empty. The woman in white had vanished yet again.

Some say she still haunts the bridge and can be seen floating to the middle of the bridge only to disappear from sight.

The locals know the area just south of the Dekalb County Line on Old Auburn Road as the Devil's Hollow. The stories surrounding the Devil's Hollow have grown over the years and include witches, an insane old man who lived on the hilltop (in some tales he's an escaped Nazi, in others he has a hook for a hand), and people hanging themselves from the trees.

A bridge near the Hollow is said to be haunted by a headless horseman (surely not the same specter transplanted from *Sleepy Hollow*!) as well as a young couple whose motorcycle skidded off the side of the bridge.

Another Devil's Hollow story concerns an old woman who lived by herself in a house on a hill. She complained to her neighbors that the local kids taunted and teased her, calling her a witch. They would vandalize her property and sneak up to look in her windows, hoping to catch sight of "the witch." The old woman loved her solitary life, but wondered if she should move somewhere else where the locals wouldn't harass her. She never got the chance. According to legend, one night some teens, sure that the old woman was a witch, burned her house to the ground, making sure that she remained inside. For years charred remains of the house stood until finally all that was left was the chimney. Now the old woman's ghost scares away those foolish enough to visit the area, feeling that the sightseers are no better than the teens that burned her to death.

Fort Wayne may or may not have been built over Indian burial grounds, but one thing is sure: there are many ghosts and legends to be found there!

Chapter Twenty
The Mean Deer
A Family's Ongoing Saga

For financial reasons, Brittney had to move her family into her mother's house. Up until then, she had never really had to deal with the paranormal. That changed soon after she moved in. Nothing creepy had ever happened in the house until they had an alarm system put in and the technician had gone into the attic to install it. Brittney doesn't know if the intrusion into the attic is what started the paranormal activity, but it's the only explanation she can think of.

Soon after the alarm system was installed, Brittney was in the living room chatting on the telephone. Her stepfather, who had just gone back to work after recovering from hernia surgery, had just left. She paused in her conversation when she realized that her son, Daniel (2 years old at the time), was softly crying. Brittney hung up and turned her attention to her son. "What's wrong? Why are you crying?"

"Pawpaw's gone and he's not coming home." Pawpaw was Daniel's name for Brittney's stepfather.

"Pawpaw's just gone to work. He'll be home in the morning," Brittney assured her son.

Daniel shook his head. "No, he's gone. He told me so."

Brittney frowned. Her first thought was that Pawpaw had confided some secret to the child. Were her mother and stepfather having problems that she knew nothing about? "Who told you he wasn't coming home? Is that what Pawpaw said?"

"No," Daniel replied. He pointed to a picture of a deer hanging on a nearby wall. "*He* told me."

"Who?" Brittney asked again, still puzzled.

"*Him!*" Daniel stabbed a finger in the direction of the painting. "Him right there!"

"Do you mean the deer in the picture?" Brittney asked.

"Yes!"

Brittney had to keep herself from smiling. Assuming this was the product of a child's imagination, she said softly, "It's just a deer in a picture, honey. It's like Bambi."

Daniel did not look convinced. "No, he's a mean deer. He looks at me like this." The boy then lowered his head, furrowed his brow, and commenced to glare at his mother.

Something about the boy's attitude caused a shudder to run down Brittney's spine. She suddenly wasn't sure this was all childish imagination. "Come here," she motioned to her son. He joined her on the couch and she held him close. Soon he fell asleep in her lap, leaving her to wonder if something odd was happening in their home.

Soon her second son, Cody, was born. As an infant in his crib, Cody was fond of staring up at a point on the ceiling and smiling as if he was watching something entertaining. The family just assumed he was a happy baby and thought no more about it. Perhaps the baby saw something others couldn't see...

Things seemed relatively quiet for a while. Cody grew and the two boys shared a bedroom. The room was a fine place to play during the day, but at night things were different. The boys were terrified of sleeping in their own room. Children often are afraid of the dark, but in her heart Brittney knew there was more to it than that.

One day Cody, now a little more than two years old, complained that someone kept tapping him on the shoulder. Thinking perhaps that it was a muscle spasm, Brittney examined his back. There was no sign of any spasm. She asked if the tapping had stopped and, smiling, Cody assured her that it had. Again, Brittney wasn't sure if the problem could be simply medical, imagination, or—and she hated to think it, but Cody's insistence worried her—some unseen presence actually tapping the boy's shoulder.

The boys' fear of their room increased. One night, Cody wanted to retrieve his blanket that he'd left in there. Brittney walked with him and entered the darkened room to show him there was nothing to be afraid of, but the boy stayed in the doorway, obviously terrified to step inside. Thinking that Cody was pretending to be afraid so he could put off going to bed, Brittney insisted that he join her at the bed. She sat and waited while the youngster slowly walked over and stood next to her. His eyes were wide with fear.

Brittney asked why he was so scared of his own room. The boy, visibly shaking, replied, "Because the boy said that this was *his* room and that we weren't allowed in it."

The next day Brittney made arrangements to switch rooms with her sons.

Every now and then Cody would again be bothered with the tapping on his shoulder. Brittney told her son that whenever the tapping occurred or the "boy" bothered him that Cody should say out loud, "Leave me alone! This is my house!" Cody followed her advice. After that Brittney would often hear her son, playing on his own, suddenly shout out, "Leave me alone!"

The boys weren't the only ones to have odd experiences. One night Brittney's mother was in bed. The rest of the family was out for the evening and she was alone in the house. Suddenly she felt the sheets being tugged at and pulled as if a small child was trying to climb up onto the bed. She decided to ignore whatever it was and turned onto her side. It then felt like something was jumping up and down on the bed next to her, although nothing was to be seen.

Brittney wanted answers. Inspired by a ghost hunting television show, she decided to try to communicate with any spirits that were in their home. Although she didn't have a digital recorder, Brittney did have an old tape recorder and she figured that would be good enough for her purposes. She asked appropriate questions and then replayed the tape. On playback, she heard what sounded like a young child saying, "You there?" The voice sounded curious and somehow sweet. Brittney played the tape for her children, not explaining what they might hear. When the child's voice sounded, the boys' faces lit up. It was a voice with which they were very familiar.

Brittney now has a daughter, Arelyn. Today Daniel and Cody are 11 and 9, respectively, and Arelyn will soon be 2. Brittney's daughter has trouble sleeping and often wakes up screaming as if she's just had a horrible dream. Brittney, taking her own advice, announces to the room as she comforts her daughter, "Leave my children alone!" This seems to work, at least for a time.

Brittney wants to have an investigation done in her home, but until that happens she'll continue to try to understand the strange occurrences that plague their house. Soon, she hopes, she'll have answers and her children can cease to be afraid in their own home.

Conclusion
A Personal Brush with the Paranormal

I have always enjoyed ghost stories, but I didn't have my *own* ghost experience until I was attending Purdue University, however. One of my best friends, Mike, had lost both of his parents and his last remaining grandparent within a short time. He had rented out his parent's house and suggested that we live off campus in the house his grandparents had lived in. It sounded like a good idea, so I packed up my few belongings and prepared for the move.

The house was fairly old and large, located near Lafayette's Columbian Park. Being poor college students, we didn't have nearly enough furniture to fill all of the rooms so we left a few of them empty. Anyone walking into the house might have thought the place was uninhabited, as the front room was bare with the exception of a rickety old hat stand.

Mike had picked the bedroom at the back of the second floor. Mine was at the opposite end, overlooking the street. The rooms in between were large and empty. We figured this way we could each play our stereos without disturbing each other. Mike's dog, a big and rather dim Doberman Pinscher, also preferred the back bedroom, since he could climb out of Mike's window and sun himself out on part of the roof! I had a large white cat named Sam that ruled the roost and he quickly taught Duke, the dog, who was boss by climbing up onto a chair and smacking him across the snout. Once the pecking order was established, the household settled down into a fairly normal routine.

I grew used to the sounds of an old house. The water pipes groaned alarmingly and the floorboards squeaked loudly with every step. The staircase leading to the second floor was particularly noisy. One couldn't take a step on it without loudly announcing your presence. Every step creaked and moaned as you put your weight down. Sneaking up to your bedroom wasn't possible.

I lived in the house for several months without even wondering if Mike, Sam, and Duke were my only house mates. True, we felt cold spots every now and then, but I thought these were caused by drafts from open windows somewhere in the house. After all, Mike usually left his window open so Duke could get out onto the roof. The house wasn't air conditioned, so windows were often left wide open.

One night I was alone in the house with only Duke and Sam for company. Mike was off playing basketball and wouldn't be back until late. As the nights were getting rather chilly, I made the rounds to ensure all windows were shut and latched. Making sure the doors were locked, I went upstairs to my bedroom to read. The dog and the cat joined me, warming my bed as I propped myself up against my headboard and started Hemingway's *The Sun Also Rises*.

Duke the dog was the first to sense something out of the ordinary. He whined and jumped off the bed, shaking with what seemed to be fear. I frowned at the dog and then noticed Sam at the foot of the bed. He'd arched his back, his hair beginning to bristle. It was then that I heard the footsteps. Someone was walking up the stairs. I waited until I heard the footsteps reach the top before saying, "Hey, Mike. Come in here. The animals are acting weird."

There was no reply.

Puzzled, I got up and looked out my bedroom door. No one was in the hall. I checked Mike's bedroom. It was empty. So were the other rooms.

I knew I had heard someone walk up the stairs. The sound was unmistakable. I was equally sure no one had walked back down. It wasn't possible to do so without making noise. Back in my bedroom, Duke was continuing to cry. Suddenly I knew that I wasn't alone in the house.

I'd always wondered what I'd do if something paranormal happened, and I found out that night. I went back to my bedroom and told the animals, "We're going for a ride."

I bundled Sam under my arm, got out Duke's leash, and headed downstairs. We made a hasty exit and I took the animals to my battered Chevy Nova. It's not easy to get a Doberman into a Nova (especially one as skittish and as excitable as Duke), but I managed it. We drove around town for an hour or so until I knew Mike would be back.

When I finally told Mike what had happened, I was surprised when he didn't laugh. Instead, he told me he'd been having strange experiences since we'd moved into the house. He hadn't told me because he thought I wouldn't believe him. Mike had been hearing footsteps as well, but had also seen an odd mist move from one of the empty bedrooms down the hall only to disappear into the other empty room. One night he'd seen what looked like crayon marks appear on the wall, only to vanish moments later. At times he felt the presence of his grandfather, and had on occasion even caught the whiff of pipe smoke. Neither Mike nor I smoked, but his grandfather had amassed a large collection of pipes and was rarely without one.

Mike, the animals, and I continued to live in the house for several years. The unseen entity stayed as well, making his or her presence known every now and then by walking up the stairs or rattling the glasses in the cupboard. We learned to live with it. My ears would always prick up whenever a visitor would say, "Something odd just happened to me." We never knew when another story would be added to our list of strange occurrences.

My fascination with ghosts and the paranormal has only increased as the years have passed.

And I'm obviously not alone. Television shows about paranormal investigating are hugely popular, and there are dozens of books about ghost hunting available. Nearly every city in every state has several ghost-hunting organizations you can join.

In Indiana, there is Crossroads Paranormal (www.crossroadsparanormal.com) and several chapters of Indiana Ghost Trackers (www.indianaghosts.org), among others. If you're interested in ghost-hunting, check out one of these organizations to see if they're currently accepting new members. These groups will ensure that you are properly trained and that your ghost hunts will be safe, exciting experiences! If you want to start up your own ghost-hunting group, be sure to check out *How to Hunt Ghosts* by Joshua P. Warren (Simon and Schuster). It provides excellent advice for the novice along with a run down of the equipment you'll need to seek out the paranormal.

Bibliography

Books:

Baker, Tom, and Jonathan Tichenal. *Haunted Indianapolis and Other Indiana Ghost Stories.* Atglen, Pennsylvania: Schiffer Publications, Ltd, 2008.

Marimen, Mark. *Haunted Indiana*. San Diego, California: Thunder Bay Press, 1997.
Haunted Indiana 2. San Diego, California: Thunder Bay Press, 1999.

Scott, Beth, and Michael Norman. *Haunted Heartland*. New York, New York: Fall River Press, 1992.

Schechter, Harold. *The Serial Killer Files*. New York, New York: Random House, 2003.

Thay, Edrick. *Ghost Stories of Indiana*. Edmonton, Alverta, Canada: Ghost House Books, 2001.

Willis, Wanda Lou. *Haunted Hoosier Trails.* Cincinnati, Ohio: Emmis Books, 2002.

Selected Websites:

http://www.chestertontribune.com/LocalHistory/alice_gray.html. "Alice Gray, Woman of the Dunes," by Vicki Urbanik.

http://wwwelkhartcivictheatre.org. "Elkhart Civic Theatre."

http://www.historicforks.org. "Forks of the Wabash."

http://www.ghostvillage.com. "Ghostvillage.com."

http://www.mlive.com. "Mlive.com."

http://munsterhistory.com. "Munsterhistory.com."

http://www.ndsmcobserver.com. "Notre Dame Observer Online."

http:www.cmgww.com/football/gipp/biography.html. "The Official George Gipp Website."

http://www.sjmed.com. "The Official Website of St. Joseph Regional Medical Center."

http://indianaghosts.org/newsletter/paranormalpress. "The Paranormal Press."

http://theshadowlands.net. "The Shadowlands."

Places Index

Bishop Noll Institute, 1519 Hoffman Street, Hammond, Indiana 46327; 112

Bristol Opera House, 210 East Vistula Street, Bristol, Indiana 46507; 97, 98

Columbia Elementary School, 1238 East Michigan Street, Hammond, Indiana 46320; 112

East Noble High School, 901 Garden Street, Kendallville, Indiana 46755; 102

Embassy Theatre, 125 West Jefferson Boulevard, Fort Wayne, Indiana 46802; 143

Ewald Cemetery, Intersection of 5A Road and Hawthorn Road, Bremen, Indiana 46506; 99

Forks of the Wabash Historic Park, Intersection of US 24 and SR 9, Huntington, Indiana 46750; 141, 156

Gavit High School, 1670 175th Street, Hammond, Indiana 46324; 112

Grand Kankakee Marsh County Park, 21690 Clay Street, Hebron, Indiana 46341; 75

158 Places Index

Hacienda Restaurant, 700 Lincolnway W, Mishawaka, Indiana 46544; 71

Highland Cemetery, 2257 ½ Portage Avenue, South Bend, Indiana 46616; 69

Holiday Inn South Bend—City Center, 213 West Washington Street, South Bend, Indiana 46601; 70

Indiana Dunes State Park, 1600 North 25 E, Chesterton, Indiana 46304; 135

Inn at Aberdeen, 3158 South State Road 2, Valparaiso, Indiana 46385; 117-123

Kaske House Museum, 1005 Ridge Road, Munster, Indiana 46321; 116-117

Oakridge Cemetery, Goshen, Indiana 46526; 46-49

Old Lighthouse Museum, 1 Washington Park Marina, Michigan City, Indiana 46360; 72

Patton Cemetery, 1401 Rumley, La Porte, Indiana 46350; 86-89

Peaceful Acres Mobile Home Park, 5485 Road 31, South Peru, Indiana 46970; 73

Posey Chapel, 1000 North 300 East, Galena, Indiana 47119; 70

Prill School Museum, 500 West 7th Street, Rochester, Indiana 46975; 104, 105

Sawmill Lake, Leesburg, Indiana 46538; 73-74

South East Grove Cemetery, 155th Street and Southgrove Road, Crown Point, Indiana; 95

St. Joseph Community Hospital, 801 East LaSalle Avenue, South Bend, Indiana 46617; 57

State Theater Lounge, 214 ½ South Michigan Street, South Bend, Indiana 46601; 70

Strand Movie Theater, 221 S. Main Street, Kendallville, Indiana 46755; 103

Tippecanoe Place Restaurant, 620 West Washington Avenue, South Bend, Indiana 46601; 7-19

University of Notre Dame, Notre Dame, Indiana 46556; 4, 12, 33-40, 156

Valparaiso University, 1700 Chapel Drive, Valparaiso, Indiana 46383; 72